JAPANESE
STYLE

JAPANESE STYLE

Designing with Nature's Beauty

Sunamita Lim

Principal Photography by
Doug Merriam

Gibbs Smith, Publisher
TO ENRICH AND INSPIRE HUMANKIND
Salt Lake City | Charleston | Santa Fe | Santa Barbara

First Edition

11 10 09 08 07   5 4 3 2 1

Published by

Gibbs Smith, Publisher

P.O. Box 667

Layton, Utah 84041

Orders: 1.800.835.4993

www.gibbs-smith.com

Designed by Ron Stucki

Printed and bound in China

Library of Congress Cataloging-in-Publication Data

Lim, Sunamita.

 Japanese style : designing with nature's beauty / Sunamita Lim. —1st

ed.

    p. cm.

 Includes bibliographical references and index.

 ISBN-13: 978-1-4236-0092-3

 ISBN-10: 1-4236-0092-4

 1. Interior decoration—Japanese influences. I. Title.

NK2115.5.E84L57 2007

745.40952—dc22

                    2007011259

The inner awakening of one's aspirations to live a humbler, more fulfilling, and beautiful Life is an act of Grace. And, the gift of realizing this aspiration by sharing it in this book is also an opportunity to express soulful Gratitude.

In a salutation to Japan after his first visit there, Sri Chinmoy said: "You offer to yourself and to the world at large what you have—the flowering of a creative spirit. You are pure because you live with Nature. You are sure because you live in faith. You have surrendered your entire existence to Beauty. You are the hyphen between imagination and transformation, between aspiration and perfection. To perceive your outer life is to feel the beauty of your heart's simplicity. To comprehend your inner life is to swim in the sea of your soul's serenity. All other nations, with no exception, will admit that your beauty without is worth invoking, and your beauty within is worth cherishing."

To Sri Chinmoy, my Indian spiritual master who has been showering me with adventures galore ever since I embarked on my inner journey in 1980, I dedicate this book. More than I can express, Sri Chinmoy's love for Japan and the world has reconnected me with the Beauty of Nature and her glorious manifestations.

CONTENTS

ACKNOWLEDGMENTS

". . . [T]he lunchbox meal is an 'art' to be eaten, just as flower arranging is an art whose appearance is modified instant by instant. . . . is it not generally the case that life waxes beautiful through energy exerted in such directions? It is not the eternal beauty of a masterpiece but rather attention to the pleasure of each passing moment that counts here. Beauty is sustained in each instant in accordance with the circumstance; the work that has been carefully built up is consumed within a constantly self-renewing canon of beauty, with its weaving in and out of history and the seasons. Within the enveloping time-space continuum, the lunchbox structure recreates beauty in daily correspondence with prevailing conditions. And thus life and society benefit from a net infusion of beauty." — KENJI EKUAN, *The Aesthetics of the Japanese Lunchbox*

Living life as a beautiful art form is clearly evident in Japan. The daily *bento*, or lunch box, is a culinary joy to behold. With its array of delicious fried cutlets, *kamaboko*, or fish cake rounds, paper-thin slices of pickled ginger, fresh vegetable salad, all spiced up with a dash of green *wasabi* (pungent horseradish paste), the *bento* is a feast for the senses.

Visually and aromatically, the *bento* box satisfies immediately. Contrasting flavors and food textures magically meld into

FACING: Drawing inspiration from similar bamboo gates in Japan, the lattice design in this gate affords a view onto the next level down.

gustatory heaven with each bite. And as each new day brings forth fresh possibilities, so too, new culinary combinations delight with each day's *bento*. Creating a *bento* lunch box and creating this book present striking parallels—from sampling Japan's impact on world cultures to partaking tidbits that lead to bigger bites of aesthetic insights to generous souls sharing their time and love for things Japanese.

Deepest gratitude is due to Sakina and Hans von Briesen, who introduced me to the intricacies of *Chado*, or the Way of Tea, and provided in-depth answers on how they built their *chaniwa*, or Japanese tea garden. And thank you to Sakina for her thoughtful review of this manuscript.

The von Briesens introduced me to Tonia Prestupa, interior designer extraordinaire. Tonia's love of Japanese culture in turn introduced me to the inimitable Mimi-san Lipps, who created breathtaking Japanese floral arrangements for photo shoots.

Arigatoo gozai masu also go to Dr. Yoko Woodson, curator of Japanese art at the Asian Art Museum in San Francisco; Duke Klauck and Deborah Fleig of Ten Thousand Waves and the use of Deborah's photos from Japan in this book; Sunrise Springs; Dale Brotherton of Takumi Carpentry; Dave Flanagan of Bamboo Fencer, Inc.; Michael Zimber of Stone Forest; Gail and Zachariah Rieke; and Mr. and Mrs. Michael Auld.

Last but not least, this elegant book owes much to principal photographer Doug Merriam's outstanding artistry, prepress specialist Jennifer Davidson's keen eye, and editor Hollie Keith's unerring yen for perfection in details and the larger picture.

To everyone—may *bento* and beauty enrich and satisfy with every delightful bite of life!

INTRODUCTION

"Simplicity is God's Beauty." — S R I   C H I N M O Y

Many appreciate the simple life. But living a life of simplicity is not simple. Rather, trying to simplify one's life is a constant challenge to embrace discipline—to edit out unnecessary items and to minimize desires that fuel their acquisition.

In *Space: Japanese Design Solutions for Compact Living* by Michael Freeman (Universe Publishing, 2004), the smallest apartment featured was a mere 200 square feet of highly organized space. (Thomas Jefferson's honeymoon

FACING: This living room in a vacation home commands a splendid view across the Columbia River near Astoria, Washington. Just as commanding is its refined *tatami* room cushioned with two-inch-thick *tatami* mats (of compacted straw fibers covered with reed); antique *shoji* room dividers on the right; new *shoji* over full-length glass doors; and the exposed, peeled bark, log roof framing of Port Orford cedar, Douglas fir beams and western red cedar for the ceiling boards. The walls are veneer plastered with a modern version of clay mixed with straw fiber. This room has been fashioned using traditional Japanese post-and-beam joinery with wedges and pins, sans hardware, with all the surfaces smoothly hand-planed. (Courtesy of Takumi Japanese Traditional Carpentry. Photography by Dale Brotherton.)

cottage was also the same size, before he moved into Monticello.[1]) With a growing population half the size of the United States but smaller than the landmass of California, Japan is an inspiration in compact living.

The Japanese admire compactness because "they feel that, like simplicity, it derives its aesthetic merit from the fact that it cannot be fully achieved without perfect execution . . . as proof of the continuing and widespread survival of a feeling for beauty among the Japanese population," Mitsukuni Yoshida explained in his essay, "Japanese Aesthetic Ideals."[2]

Thus challenged, the Japanese ethos thrives on creative ways for doing more with less.

Added to this are seasonal fluxes necessitating changes in décor—all of which drive a constant state of dynamic renewal. And the preciousness of fleeting moments brings home the saying, *ichi-go ichi-e*, meaning "each meeting only once," in celebrating the uniqueness of each *chanoyu*, or tea ceremony, and indeed, of every moment.

Dr. Yoko Woodson, curator of Japanese art at San Francisco's Asian Art Museum, commented to me, "Nonattachment is a subtle but strong quality in Japanese culture." The evanescence of life as symbolized by the intense flowering of cherry blossoms for only one week after a whole year's preparation is symbolic of ephemeral beauty.

So, why do we unwittingly complicate our lives? Let us instead enjoy a beautiful life.

For a life of luxury is, after all, a life of simplicity—by being free of unnecessary encumbrances. And, living in beauty is simply living deeply in the soul's true beauty.

The goal of this book is for ongoing serendipitous discoveries each time you pause, and reflect, on these pages—and for enrichment in whatever direction your heart takes you.

[1] Rybczynski, *The Most Beautiful House in the World*, 137.
[2] *In Japan Style*, the Japan Foundation's catalog for this exhibition at the Victoria and Albert Museum in London, 21.

The plain Amish chest of drawers on the left is a perfect foil for artist Gail Rieke's collection of collections—from keys to colorful matchbox labels to fish traps.

A LIFESTYLE COMMENTARY ON JAPANESE AESTHETICS

"Yes, it isn't every grocery store that pays tribute to beauty and spends millions in the process. But it's the Japanese way to provide a clean, good, safe environment for our customers."

— TOMOKO MORIGUCHI-MATSUNO, Uwajimaya Food and Gifts, Seattle

"I do not believe architecture should speak too much. It should remain silent and let Nature in the guise of sunlight and wind speak," said Tadao Ando, Japan's world-renowned architect.[1] Ando, admired for his flowing designs playing on light and sublime shadows encased in the spare minimalism of clean, concrete forms, gently invites nature into his buildings, be they residential or commercial.

Awarded the Pritzker Architecture Prize in 1995, which is the Nobel equivalent in the industry, this self-taught architect is a professional paradox because Ando did not go to architecture school nor acquire a degree (although

---

[1] www.pritzkerprize.com/andorel.htm#Ando's.

he's received many honorary degrees and distinguished honors now).

Instead, this introspective architect mastered the traditional art of Japanese wood designing and building first. Ando lived across from a woodworking shop while growing up in Osaka, Japan. In the time-honored Japanese tradition of studying from the masters, he learned the precision techniques required in building with wood joinery, sans hardware, so tightly and expertly that no water would seep through. Building on these wood-crafting skills, Ando designs his signature "smooth-as-silk" concrete structures. Tadao Ando is lauded for his skillful artistry in combining the art of designing on a human scale with the art of building durable dwellings, inspiring occupants fortunate to be living in the spaces designed by him.

People ask if it's the smoothness of the concrete he uses, but it all comes down to the perfectionism of fine Japanese craftsmanship—and Ando's genius in applying these principles to building in another medium, concrete. In a similar vein, Japanese master potters expertly slump, or throw, clay to result in exquisitely fine pieces, regardless of the nature of the clay used.

When I first saw photographs of Ando's "Church on the Water" located in Hokkaido, Japan, my heart almost stopped beating. You can see why by visiting the Web site in the footnote on the previous page. Nestled in early fall foliage, the exterior shot is peaceful and bucolic. However, the interior shot cloaked in winter's ethereal light and celestial whiteness all but transcends heaven on earth with a realistic, yet surrealistic, cross serenely standing in and commanding the still, pure waters. Ando explained, "By placing a cross in a body of flowing water, I wanted to express the idea of

BELOW: Taos Mountain, New Mexico, provides a compelling backdrop for the gate to a Japanese-style home designed by Aaron Bohrer. (Photography by Robert Reck.)

BOTTOM: Here is a view of this same Taos home from the mountains. (Photography by Robert Reck.)

BELOW: The dressing alcove is an elegant design that conceals a walk-in closet and storage cabinets, heightened by the stylistic placement of the *tokobasira* to the right.

God as existing in one's heart and mind. I also wanted to create a space where one can sit and meditate."[2]

Intrigued, I asked Dale Brotherton, a Japanese-trained master designer/builder since 1987 and founder of Takumi Japanese Carpentry, why Americans are so fascinated by Japanese-style architecture and the demand for his services. "It is both calming and enriching to experience a home environment that's designed Japanese style," Brotherton said. "Most people cannot verbalize why, or even what, inspires that experience. They only know that they desire it for their own homes. It is up to the designer/builder to create it for them. This is an inherent skill of the Japanese builder—to discern homeowner tastes and desires that are unexpressed for the most part, and then marry these aspirations to the designer/builder's skill and experience in creating an appropriate dwelling," he continued. Takumi Company (www.japanesecarpentry.com) is located in north Seattle.

The respectful status accorded master craftsmen underscores their importance in a society that, up to a century and a half ago, built dwellings primarily of wood, clay, straw, and paper.

The cultural trait of honoring humanity and the environment is so ingrained in Japanese society that it bears sharing this amazing feat of architectural design. On January 17, 1995, a devastating earthquake measuring 7.2 on the Richter scale hit the city of Kobe in Japan. Hundreds and thousands were left homeless in this city of 1.5 million, with losses at more than $100 million. Yet the thirty-plus buildings designed and built by Tadao Ando survived, including the Water Temple on Awaji Island at the center of the fault line.

[2] Ibid.

BELOW: A *tsukabai*, or hollowed rock basin, holds fresh water for tea ceremony guests or temple devotees to rinse their mouths and to wash their hands before entering the inner sanctum. The traditional dipper, *hisaku*, is made of bamboo. (Courtesy of Golden Door, Escondido, California.)
FACING: The warm assemblage of colorful tapestry, vibrant bamboo plant, and burnished wood stairs transports visitors to Japan as they walk up to the reception area at Ten Thousand Waves.

By listening to Nature, Tadao Ando has realized the highest depths of spiritual truth to build appropriately—via accessing inner light with his meditation—so that architecture remains mute, to better allow "nature in the guise of sunlight and wind [to] speak."

For his part, Ando was smitten with Shaker furniture on his first visit to the United States. "I was astounded by the freshness of [Shaker] wooden furniture. . . . The mood of the pieces was simple and reserved and exerted a restraining and ordering effect on the surroundings. Technically, the furniture was rationally made with no waste of any kind. . . . In the great diversity of modern times, to experience objects representing an extreme simplification of life and form was very refreshing."[3]

In another exchange of design sentiments between Japan and America, a seventeen-year-old Tadao Ando was struck by Frank Lloyd Wright's redesign of Tokyo's Imperial Hotel, which took ten years to construct, from 1913 to 1923. Ando identified with Wright's spatial designs manifesting inherently Japanese sensibilities. "I had never heard of him, nor did I know anything about the building. But the Imperial Hotel fascinated me and my curiosity took me inside. I remember a dark, narrow corridor with an extremely low ceiling leading into a huge hall. It was like walking through a cave. I think Wright learned the most important aspect of architecture, the treatment of space, from Japanese architecture. When I visited Falling Water in Pennsylvania, I found that same sensibility of space. But there was the additional natural sounds of nature that appealed to me," Ando was quoted as saying on the Pritzker Prize Web site, www.pritzkerprize.com.[4]

Wright had composed "A Song to Heaven" in his 1932

---

[3] Lawrence, *The Wabi-Sabi House*, 75.

[4] However, Swiss-born French architect Le Corbusier is Ando's main muse. Ando named his dog after him.

An Autobiography, waxing poetic on "spiritual lessons the East has power to teach the West." Wright declared "the native home in Japan . . . a supreme study in elimination—not only of dirt but the elimination of the insignificant." He saw straw-thatched Japanese villages clustering the mountainsides, looking as natural as birds nesting in trees. "By heaven, here was a house used by those who made it with just that naturalness with which a turtle uses his shell," Wright enthused,[5] thus igniting an epiphany to promote "organic architecture."

[5] Stewart, *The Making of a Modern Japanese Architecture,* 85.

"Wright sought to develop a unique brand of organic architecture in which both form and materials were one with the site," wrote Alexandra Black in *The Japanese House*.[6] Black wrote that Wright incorporated Japanese design sensibilities into his projects with "interior flow, the open floor plan and the dissolving of the boundaries between inside and outside elements . . . [and] updating the Japanese device of sliding wooden screens, which can be pulled back to merge indoor and outdoor spaces." She also noted "Wright's pioneering use of textured concrete" as part of his innovations in going organic.

David B. Stewart reported Wright was also infatuated with Japanese *ukiyo-e* art, wood block prints depicting nonaristocratic activities and teahouse dalliances with courtesans, and that he became a passionate collector, and also traded these prints.[7]

Stewart deduced in his book, *The Making of a Modern Japanese Architecture: 1868 to the Present*, that Wright's life-long affinity for nature was indelibly catalyzed from his first visit to Japan in 1905. Three years later, imbued with another Japanese design sensibility, Wright declared, "The basis of the *new style*, and henceforth of 'style' itself, must be 'SIMPLICITY.'"[8]

Japanese culture has always been a source of inspiration and mystery for Americans, and vice versa for the Japanese, as well. My hope is for readers to glean refreshing insights on the Japanese lifestyle to enhance their homes and gardens, plus to discover inspirations for daily living while contemplating the pages of this book.

---

[6] Black, 164–65.

[7] Stewart, 74.

[8] Ibid.

2

WHAT IS JAPANESE STYLE TO AMERICANS?

"Shibui beauty, the beauty of the Tea Ceremony, is beauty that makes an artist of the viewer." — SOETSU YANAGI

The Allure of "Japanese Style"

It's easy to see why Americans and Europeans are attracted to the Zen-like simplicity of Japanese interiors because the spare, neat rooms invite silent reflection while offering tranquil repose in return. Plus, looking at a serene garden setting in varying shades of green is a refreshing change of scenery from the daily grind. Japanese interiors also provide sanctuary from a chaotic world at the end of the day, thus gifting inner renewal to soul and spirit and, consequently, for outer mind and body too.

Over the course of centuries, Japan's sociocultural development has been influenced by Chinese design and garden styles. But the singular trait of Japanese ingenuity is one that modifies and adapts new imported ideas to

FACING: Craftsman-like elements of lamp and post design draw inspiration from the sparse yet elegant simplicity of Zen. The gentle climb is reason to pause and ponder, taking deliberately meditative steps towards the destination.

"Japan is a country filled with infinite beauty. It has an image of a beautiful flower garden. This beauty is expressed through inner peace. Man has seen many things, but of these things, peace is new. Japan is offering this new treasure to the world." — S R I   C H I N M O Y , *Japan: Soul-Beauty's Heart-Garden*

result in styles that are uniquely, and distinctively, Japanese.

The Japanese have traditionally connected with nature and the universe via meditation, a conscious way of accessing inner wealth to build on outer wealth. By going with the universal flow as it were, the Japanese build with, and not against, nature. Similar to Chinese feng shui, the Japanese embrace *fusui*, instinctively resulting in structures blessed with a natural serenity when situated harmoniously with the terrain and tapping into natural light.

Meditation as a lifestyle practice, such as through *Chado*, or the Way of Tea, intuits deeper insights for practical applications to daily living for many Japanese.

It's worth noting that, like most cultures, Japan took a material turn after World War II. But as Kenzo Tange, the architect in charge of rebuilding Hiroshima after the war ended, said, "In the 1970's, because of the energy crisis, our values—at least in Japan—shifted from material things to the non-physical, and even spiritual considerations.

"With de-emphasis on industrialization and the advent of the 'information-communication society,' the fundamentally rational and functional philosophy of the preceding period changed, and people sought things that appeal to the emotions and the senses. In architecture, the demand was no longer for box-like forms, but for buildings that have something to say to the human emotions. That new

demand has had an effect on the designs of everything, from small window displays to streetscapes to buildings," Tange noted in his acceptance speech, upon becoming the first Japanese to be honored with the Pritzker Architecture Prize in 1987, architecture's equivalent of the Nobel Prize.[1]

A major reason that explains Japan's openness in welcoming and adapting innovations is this pearl from Tange's acceptance speech, which describes how the past is honored as new ideas emerge: "Creative work is expressed in our time as a union of technology and humanity. The role of tradition is that of a catalyst, which furthers a chemical reaction, but is no longer detectable in the end result. Tradition can, to be sure, participate in a creation, but it can no longer be creative itself."

One of Kenzo Tange's students was Tadao Ando, and both men were immensely inspired by the design vision and

[1] www.pritzkerprize.com.

mission of Swiss-born French architect Le Corbusier (whose impact on Modernist architecture with clean, sculptural designs using newer materials of concrete and metals is legendary around the world).

In the 1920s, Le Corbusier revolutionized the design world with his architectural theory of building with a piling system to absorb and distribute the weight of the structure and walls, rooftop garden terraces, an open-plan floor space, continuous windows to light up interiors with natural light and sunlight, and freedom in designing the façade.[2]

But where the Japanese parted ways with "Corbu" is their success in humanizing homes, which Le Corbusier called "machines for living."

By scaling space to Japanese proportions and sensibilities, and by showcasing the cultural appreciation for nuances of light and shadow play in a room, these designers magically evoke a precious Japanese aesthetic—of "an inexpressible aura of depth and mystery, of overtones but partly suggested"[3]—and the essence of *yugen*, which hints of deeper mysteries to uncover. A person is thus emotionally moved, and inexplicably so; while on deeper levels, mystical experiences intensify. It's similar to being moved by candlelight, flickering shadows, and the mysterious glows emanating from a burning log fire, from the very depths of the soul.

Jun' Ichiro Tanizaki wrote in his book, *In Praise of Shadows*, "The quality that we call beauty, however, must always grow from the realities of life, and our ancestors, forced to live in dark rooms, presently came to discover beauty in shadows, ultimately to guide shadows towards beauty's ends.

"And so it has come to be that the beauty of a Japanese room depends on a variation of shadows, heavy shadows against light shadows—it has nothing else. Westerners are amazed at the simplicity of Japanese rooms, perceiving in them no more than ashen walls bereft of ornament. Their reaction is understandable, but it betrays a failure to comprehend the mystery of shadows."[4]

"Traditional Japanese arts are among the richest in the world. They are also among the most elusive. Few peoples have cared longer or more deeply about beauty than the Japanese, but they have written about it in most cases obliquely, relying on the arts themselves to convey their own expressive charge."[5]

---

[2] Asensio, ed. *Le Corbusier*, 6.

[3] Tanizaki, *In Praise of Shadows*, 14.

[4] Ibid.

[5] Addiss, Stephen, et al., *Traditional Japanese Arts and Culture*, 1.

"Space and light and order. Those are the things that men need just as much as they need bread or a place to sleep." — L E C O R B U S I E R

"Fundamentally, human beings, whether Eastern or Western, need belief, free play of imagination and intuition in their homes and workshops or they become starved. All the cog-wheels and electronic brains cannot assuage these human needs in the long run." — B E R N A R D   L E A C H , in his introduction to Soetsu Yanagi's *The Unknown Craftsman: A Japanese Insight Into Beauty*

The Natural Beauty of Inner Radiance: Wabi Sabi and Shibui

Another Japanese attribute not easily articulated, even by the Japanese themselves, is the notion of *wabi sabi*, made all the more attractive by the very nature of its elusiveness. And even more quietly restrained is the aesthetic quality of *shibui*. As a Zen Buddhist *koan*, or conundrum, muses: that which is, may not be so; while that which appears not (especially in an understated way) is "the real McCoy."

Not exclusive to being applied in any one domain, *wabi sabi* and *shibui* pervade all facets of Japanese life, as the observations below illustrate.

"*Wabi* is quiet serenity, a silence that is deep and profound—and sometimes mistaken for loneliness. But it is a deep silence that enriches the person with self-discovery," said Dr. Yoko Woodson, curator of Japanese art at San Francisco's Asian Art Museum. "*Sabi* is rusticity, and a closeness to the naturalness of nature," Woodson continued.

"Japanese culture celebrates layers of contrasts and diversity. For example, *hade* is showy and ostentatious, as in dressing up a kimono with colors and ornamentation. The opposite is *jimi,* where dressing down a kimono results in a

more subdued and toned-down appearance. Depending on the occasion, we express our emotions in appropriate ways of dressing," Woodson explained.

Married to an American and living in the United States, Yoko Woodson is often called on to explain the reason for *wabi sabi*. Pausing, she said, "Nonattachment is a subtle but strong quality in Japanese culture." Using the cherry blossom as metaphor, Woodson proffered, "The brief one week that it blossoms is a precious time to view, and appreciate, its beauty. We call this eagerly anticipated event *hanami*. It takes a whole year's preparation for the cherry blossom to bloom, only to be dissolved by the wind into a snowfall of petals on the ground."

Hence, given life's impermanence (*mujo*), fleeting moments of beauty are treasured all the more—but with total nonattachment and a deep feeling of gratitude. "The fact of impermanence now becomes a spiritual and an aesthetic value, producing in a sensitive person the possibility of a sense for beauty deriving from an inevitable self-awareness concerning one's own evanescence," noted Yoshida Kenzo in his "Essays on Idleness."[6]

In his essay "The Wabi Aesthetic Through the Ages," Haga Koshiro describes three intrinsic properties of *wabi*. First, "*wabi* means to transform material insufficiency so that one

[6] Addiss, et. al. *Traditional Japanese Arts and Culture*, 85.

discovers in it a world of spiritual freedom unbounded by material things. It means not being trapped by worldly values but finding a transcendental serenity apart from the world." Second, "the incomplete is clearly more beautiful than the perfect . . . [in finding] a deeper beauty in the blemished than in the unblemished . . . further explained as lacking essential parity, being asymmetrical, unbalanced . . . [and] irregular." Third, the "austere beauty of age and experience, which can only be attained through a master's accomplishment, to be the epitome of beauty."[7]

In making cross-cultural comparisons, British author Andrew Juniper wrote, "The term *wabi sabi* suggests such qualities as impermanence, humility, asymmetry, and imperfection. These underlying principles are diametrically opposed to those of their Western counterparts, whose values are rooted in a Hellenic worldview that values permanence, grandeur, symmetry, and perfection.

"Japanese art, infused with the spirit of *wabi sabi*, seeks beauty in the truths of the natural world, looking towards nature for its inspiration. It refrains from all forms of intellectual entanglement, self-regard, and affectation in order to discover the unadorned truth of nature. Since nature can be defined by its asymmetry and random imperfections, *wabi sabi* seeks the purity of natural imperfection."[8]

When asked what appeals most to him in designing and building traditional Japanese-style structures, master wood builder Dale Brotherton replied, "*Wabi sabi. Wabi* is tasteful, restrained, and refined. *Sabi* is rustic simplicity. Combined together, they embody the character of most traditional Japanese crafts in using available materials that are care-

---

[7] Koshiro, "The Wabi Aesthetic through the Ages," in *A Reader in Japanese Aesthetics and Culture*, 254–76.

[8] Juniper, *Wabi Sabi: The Japanese Art of Impermanence*, 2.

fully crafted with simple, uncluttered designs highlighting the natural beauty of the materials used."

But going even beyond *wabi sabi* is the deeper aesthetic concept of *shibui*, discussed by the father of the Japanese and Korean craft movement, Soetsu Yanagi, in his book, *The Unknown Craftsman: A Japanese Insight into Beauty*. Regarded as the ultimate connoisseur of Japanese crafts, Soetsu Yanagi founded two folk art museums to preserve these treasures—in Korea and in Japan. His close friend, the English potter Bernard Leach (author of the renowned *A Potter's Book*), compiled some of Yanagi's prolific writings in a posthumous tribute to Yanagi in *The Unknown Craftsman*. Bernard Leach was Soetsu Yanagi's dear friend of fifty years.

Yanagi, reported Leach, discusses beauty predicated on which a "certain love of roughness is involved, behind which lurks a hidden beauty, to which we refer in our peculiar adjectives *shibui, wabi,* and *sabi*. Tea-bowls are not a project of the intellect. Yet their beauty is well-defined, which is why it has been referred to both as the beauty of the imperfect and the beauty that deliberately rejects the perfect. Either way, it is a beauty lurking within. It is this beauty with inner implications that is referred to as *shibui*.

"It is not a beauty displayed before the viewer by its creator; creation here means, rather, making a piece that will lead the viewer to draw beauty out for himself. In this sense, *shibui* beauty, the beauty of the Tea ceremony, is beauty that makes an artist of the viewer."[9]

Further expounding on *shibui* with regard to the tea ceremony, Yanagi said, "Many words were invented to describe the beauty that was to be the final criterion, and of them all perhaps the most suggestive is the adjective *shibui* (with the noun *shibusa*), for which there is no exact English counterpart. Nearest to it, perhaps, are such adjectives as "austere," "subdued," and "restrained"; but to the Japanese, the word is more complex, suggesting quietness, depth, simplicity, and purity. The beauty it describes is introversive, the beauty of the inner radiance. Another way of approaching its meaning is to consider its antonyms: "showy," "gaudy," "boastful," and "vulgar."[10]

[9] Soetsu Yanagi, 123–24.
[10] Ibid., 148.

ABOVE: The natural rusticity, or *wabi sabi*, of this teahouse at Sunrise Springs is heightened by the use of natural logs, rocks, and stone. (Photography by Kim Kurian.)

A cosmopolitan aesthete who was also deeply spiritual, Yanagi had immersed himself in Christian mysticism when he was young, and wrote a book on the English poet-mystic William Blake. In his search for truth, Yanagi urged, "Those men of Tea savoured implements from the point of view of beauty; but although their outlook may be called depth in appreciation, it cannot be called depth of *cognition* for those of us who live in a conscious age. Together with seeing beauty, we want to understand the truth behind it. We are concerned with the principles that cause beauty. Especially today, we reflect upon the social background that made such beauty possible. We do not remain on the level of appreciation alone, for we are urged on in the search for truth. Thus our observation of the past leads us towards a creative future."[11]

Yanagi was ahead of his time. In a poignant commentary filled with sad irony, Yanagi invited the Tokyo National Museum, devoid of folk arts then, to consider his personal collection of Japanese crafts as a gift in the mid-1920s, "but whether they attached no value to the objects as such or simply had not the space, there was no reply at all."[12]

The upside to this rejection, though, was Yanagi founding the Japan Folkcraft Museum, Mingeikan, in Tokyo in 1935. He also coined the term *mingei* (meaning "art of the people"), to honor the myriad anonymous men and women who crafted treasures born of their love for discovering beauty in working with natural materials.

It's important to iterate Yanagi's concern not only for art to be appreciated with a fine cognitive eye, but also for art to be relevant with comfort and utility for the end users. In a similar vein, architect-designer Charles Eames and his wife, Ray, contributed to the new design movement in the United States from their Santa Monica home in California.

[11] Ibid., 213–14.
[12] Ibid., 102.

Their classic Eames Lounge Chair and Ottoman celebrated its fiftieth anniversary in 2006.

Yanagi and Leach had met with the Eameses at their home in 1954. The two men were inspired by Charles Eames' "open acceptance both of the contemporary science and industrial world as well the traditions of the past, upon his playful refusal to be chained by fear, and his constant inventiveness and domination of the mechanical by a new freedom of intuition and joy in making."[13]

In his homage to his father, Sori Yanagi's essay "The Discovery of Beauty: Soetsu Yanagi and Folkcrafts," in *Mingei: Masterpieces of Japanese Folkcraft*, reiterates the senior Yanagi's belief that "the beauty of folk crafts is the beauty of 'naturalness and health,'" a process of artistic intent that is "spontaneous, unconscious, and vigorous, arising out of devotion to function . . . [where] use equals beauty. . . . For beautiful things to be made, not only the makers but the users and the entire distribution network must be healthy. Beauty is inseparable from *yo*, meaning function or use . . . a word that embraces the mental or spiritual dimensions of human life. . . ."[14]

Yanagi might have enjoyed visiting Shibui Gallery in Santa Fe, New Mexico. Owner Dane Owen had inadvertently named it so, having been smitten after reading about

---

[13] Ibid., 96.
[14] Sori Yanagi, 29–32.

BELOW: The natural simplicity of this *tokonoma* imparts a mysterious mood with its gray clay slip. (Photography by Kimon D. Lightner.)
BOTTOM: A close-up of the *tokonoma*'s screen, woven of twigs and bamboo. (Photography by Kimon D. Lightner.)

shibui. House Beautiful editor Elizabeth Gordon had devoted both the August and September 1960 issues to the concept.[15] On his Web site, www.shibuihome.com, Owen admits his derring-do in wearing his heart on his sleeve by naming his gallery thus. Why? Because it goes against the very grain of *shibui* to be so forthright with one's emotions.

Also on Owen's Web site are some salient points from *House Beautiful*'s August 1960 issue: "*Shibui* describes a profound, unassuming, quiet feeling. It is unobtrusive and unostentatious. It may have hidden attainments, but they are not paraded or displayed. The form is simple and must have been arrived at with an economy of means. *Shibui* is never complicated or contrived. . . . A thing *shibui* must have depth worth studying after first being noticed. It must not reveal itself all at once. It is interesting, with intrinsic quality and depth of character. Its beauty is imperfect and unique, enhanced by particularities. . . . *Shibui* is the essence of controlled understatement, and requires an attitude of modesty and humility."

The Grace of Natural Style

Nature's unaffected beauty constantly inspires, gracefully and effortlessly. *Wabi sabi* and *shibui* command attention with their qualities of elegant simplicity, subtle profundity, unobtrusiveness, quiet majesty, understated dignity, refined restraint, and timeless appeal—an altogether pleasing aesthetic on both inner and outer planes.

No wonder Japanese-style design and building has garnered such worldwide attention in the face of modernization. Soetsu Yanagi astutely noted, "As we all know, America is the home of the machine . . . yet, ever since the war, it is there that a new move towards handwork has taken

---

[15] Dane Owen's mother, Susan Owen, had saved them and given them to her son two years ago. She is especially struck by Japan's clean cities and their surroundings; and how "unflashy and unassuming the Japanese people are."

place. Even the universities are teaching handcrafts as part of their curricula, especially pottery and weaving. Why has this strange thing happened? England started the Industrial Revolution (in the 1830s), and the beauty of products deteriorated. In protest, William Morris's arts and crafts movement arose and spread all over Europe. Again why did this happen? The answer is that so many shoddy and badly designed goods caused protest."[16]

And Beauty by way of good design transcends cultural boundaries, as shown by Leach and Yanagi and the architects Tadao Ando and Frank Lloyd Wright. In a society that has celebrated a long history of honoring this natural inclination to create with natural grace, the mere act of trying to verbalize *wabi sabi* and *shibui* is, paradoxically, an elusive one—except by the powerful, outer expressions of Japanese arts in such areas as architecture, the tea ceremony (*chanoyu*) and ceramics.

Certainly, our attraction to Japanese-style structures, interiors, and gardens reflects a universal desire to live in natural harmony with self, others, and the world—where the home environment reflects soulful sentiments of simplicity, sincerity, humility, and purity; that continuously refresh spirit, emotions, and body; and where every item performs at least one useful function, if not more, and is comfortable to the touch.

The next chapter shows how simple, understated interiors are subtle sources of quiet energy that constantly rejuvenate; how practical steps for living in harmony with nature reward immeasurably; how recognizing the humility of living with, and in, a universe espoused by Frank Lloyd Wright is "too vast and intimate and real for the mere intellect to seize"[17]; and how purity in design, with form following function gracefully, is exemplified by the exquisite woodworking examples found in Japanese homes and furniture.

[16] Soetsu Yanagi, *The Unknown Craftsman*, 107.
[17] Stewart, *The Making of a Modern Japanese Architecture*, 75.

BELOW: The *tokonoma*, or sacred alcove, inside Sunrise Springs teahouse. The mud-plastered wall finish provides a naturally elegant *wabi sabi* texture. The *washi*-covered lower section of the wall protects guests' kimonos. (Courtesy of Sunrise Springs.)

BOTTOM: This Taos, New Mexico, home prevails on passive cooling and heating with a Japanese-style dry garden courtyard; the high-desert conditions encouraging a xeriscaped border along one wall. (Photography by Robert Reck.)

3 MEDITATIONS ON BEAUTY IN JAPAN

"In the East the foundation is in the heart and its inspiration, which to the Western mind, with its emphasis on the intellect, must appear very strange, for Eastern man jumps to his conclusions on wings of intuition." — SOETSU YANAGI

In the previous chapter, we discussed how grace notes of natural beauty strike common chords of appreciation with both Americans and Japanese. In *House Beautiful*'s August 1960 issue, editor Elizabeth Gordon asked readers: "Why an issue on Japan? Our answer is simple. It is worth doing if it helps you exercise new muscles of awareness, if it opens your eyes. . . . Furthermore, we share many common interests, because for centuries, they have been living more nearly as we do in suburban America—in separate houses surrounded by private gardens, designed to perform as extensions of the rooms from which they are viewed."[1]

---

[1] Gordon, 53.

"All works of art, it may be said, are more beautiful when they suggest something beyond themselves than when they end up being merely what they are." —S O E T S U   Y A N A G I , *The Unknown Craftsman: A Japanese Insight Into Beauty*

More importantly, Gordon finds a "non-separation of the beautiful from the practical" in the Japanese aesthetic. In her article "We Invite You to Enter a New Dimension: *Shibui*," Gordon extolled *shibui*'s virtues: from being "simple with an economy of line and effort"; to new items not being shiny, "although small touches of sparkle are okay"; to the "dull patina that comes with loving care" to achieve—the ultimate in taste.[2]

Mitsukuni Yoshida, in his essay on the nuances of "Japanese Aesthetic Ideals," explained, "Simplicity cannot be successful unless it is supported by perfection of craftsmanship; complexity, on the other hand, has on occasion served in attempts to cover up imperfection."[3]

Along with simplicity is the Japanese custom of appreciating the beauty of raw materials, wherein an "apparent dominance of the material of the work of art over the carefully reticent hand of the artist" is a heartfelt tribute to truth in beauty. "The inherent and natural inclinations of clay, ash, wood, bamboo, lacquer, and fiber are respected and encouraged to become major factors influencing the appearance and design of artifacts," Sherman E. Lee wrote in *The Genius of Japanese Design*.[4]

---

[2] Ibid., 120.

[3] In The Japan Foundation's Exhibition Catalogue for the Victoria and Albert Museum's Japan Style exhibit in London, 1980, 21.

[4] Lee, 10–11.

Additionally, a soft voice of humility, or *kenkyo,* is dominant in the Japanese character—a quality that makes it all the more powerful, given humility's understated presence. In describing a society predicated on mutual help and group consensus, British author Andrew Juniper explained, "The Japanese have never been a race to tolerate those who wish to appear different or better. This finds voice in the Japanese saying 'The nail that stands up will be hit down.'

Humility with your fellowmen and humility in the face of the powers that guide our lives is a much-admired attribute in Japanese society."[5]

Juniper continues, "A Japanese carpenter for instance will treat his tools and the materials he uses with an intense reverence. His function is to try his best to bring out the wood's inner beauty in a harmonious way. When his work is done he will not be seeking praise or gratitude for the

[5] Juniper, *Wabi Sabi: The Japanese Art of Impermanence,* 56.

The Zen-like simplicity of the living room is offset by the owners' collection of colorful tinplates in the kitchen.

work, for he has a personal sense of satisfaction that he has done his best and can do no more.

"This sense of modesty is the lifeblood of *wabi sabi* and saves the work of artists from being tainted by the pretensions or ambitions of an artist. *Wabi sabi* art must have this essential element of humility if it is to retain the purity of its spirit," Juniper wrote.[6]

Such caring attention to artistic detail and personal modesty can only contribute to a refined state of perfection in craftsmanship that elevates handcrafts to the level of fine arts in Japan. In her humility, the craftswoman recognizes that she is not a lone instrument expressing the divine act of creation.

"For this reason, the tools that help a man in his work and that extend the range of what he can do are often personified and regarded as having life and suffering death in the same way as a man. The date on which a tool was first used is often recorded in writing on its surface—this is the day the tool came to life. And when the tool has been in use for a long time and is no longer serviceable, it is ceremonially buried," Mitsukuni Yoshida explained.[7]

The ultimate compliment on how beauty affects human behavior comes from former *House Beautiful* editor Elizabeth Gordon: "The Japanese have an almost childlike idealism that one should find delight in everything.

"They have acquired eyes and ears that hear so they enjoy, as Bernard Leach has expressed it, 'all that pertains to beauty and poetic insight in the things of the house—

[6] Ibid. 57.
[7] Yoshida, *Japan Style*, 22.

FACING: The beautiful symmetry of planed wood is revealed in the simple linear designs of two complementary Japanese doorways. (Courtesy of Ten Thousand Waves. Photography by Deborah Fleig.)

BELOW: The gracious lobby of Golden Door spa has translucent sliding *shoji* screens to moderate light diffusing in from the outside. (Courtesy of Golden Door, Escondido, California.)

pottery, painting, calligraphy, lacquer, food, flowers, movement—human relationship itself.'"[8]

Going with the Japanese saying that a picture is worth a thousand words, the four sections in this chapter will present opportunities to see and to go beyond the obvious in appreciating some finer elements of Japanese style. In the manner of *shibui*, whatever moves you is an intimate discovery of simple and direct ways of looking at, and connecting with, beauty on your own turf.

Simplicity in Style— Refined Interiors Refresh

In the previous chapter, we noted Jun' Ichiro Tanizaki's remark, "Westerners are amazed at the simplicity of Japanese rooms." But going beyond this initial perception, many are filled with a deeper awareness that, indeed, less is more when empty space becomes an understated element of room design, thanks to disciplined editing.

By nature, the Japanese are disciplined and restrained in showing emotions, and this cultural trait is reflected in their careful editing of details, in every movement, and in everything that they do.

And by telling us that simplicity cannot be successful unless supported by perfectionism in craftsmanship, Mitsukuni Yoshida brings home the true beauty of Japanese interiors enriched by details, as in the fine carving of a *ranma* transom, the exquisite cabinetry of a *tansu*, or chest, and the design element of empty space pulsating with silent energy, prompting Frank Lloyd Wright to call for "the elimination of the insignificant."

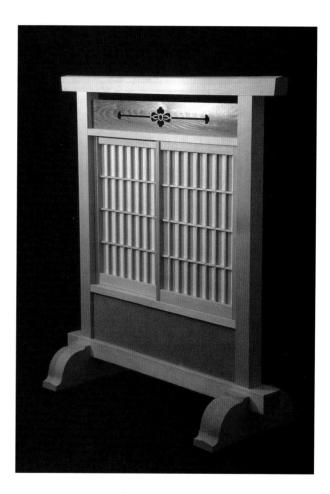

Sincerity in Nature— A Tribute to Naturalness

Japanese *fusui* is similar to Chinese feng shui in tuning in to the natural flow of cosmic energy to invigorate the senses. Nature's meditation on garden and sky is but a simple act of taking time out for quiet time, to clarify and purify emotions, and to access illumination and enrichment from deep within.

[8] Gordon, *House Beautiful*, 119.

"Simplicity and humility are of supreme importance in life. Japan has them both . . . no other country has simplicity and a heart of humility in the pure sense that Japan has." — S R I   C H I N M O Y ,

Japan: Soul-Beauty's Heart-Garden

Japanese homes with their open floor plans recognize the importance of ventilation, continuously reenergizing the room with fresh new energy by welcoming in breezes to flow unobstructed. During the warmer months, *fusuma*, or sliding screen doors, are moved back, thus enabling interior spaces to connect with the garden and nature (or wind and light, as Tadao Ando puts it).

This also expands room space to include the *engawa*, or

veranda, the transitional wraparound space extending to the garden that doubles as an extra room for various activities, from sewing to entertaining—and seamlessly connecting residents and guests with the garden. (Incidentally, the *engawa* has not been without influence on the development of the bungalow house style.)

Humility to Honor—The Teahouse Soulfully Nurtures

When I was invited to enter a Japanese teahouse on the grounds of Sunrise Springs Resort and Spa in Santa Fe, New Mexico, by crawling through a low, square doorway to participate in a *chanoyu,* or tea ceremony, it was an awkward moment. But it was also a revelatory moment to pause and ponder.

And that's precisely the function of this small doorway, originally intended for *samurai* warriors to leave behind their swords, prostrate themselves in an act of humility, and be nourished and healed in spirit by participating in the *chanoyu.*

It was a rare moment indeed—to slip off my shoes, self-consciously aware of crawling in, and then to compose myself. Natsuko Yamamoto, the tea ceremony hostess, was gracious in her welcome. She proffered a round cushion filled tightly with straw, which turned out to be good support for sitting cross-legged on the *tatami* straw mat.

Ordinarily, taking time to enjoy a cup of tea is a revitalizing activity to restore anyone's energy. However, participating in a *chanoyu* orchestrated with formal steps was a memorable experience to reflect on experiencing beauty

of a different kind—in movements a harried person might find exaggerated, but were quietly meditative to me.

Yamamoto was a study in the artistry of movements both direct and spare, from tea preparation to serving it with élan. And as a fortunate guest, I was humbled to be served so sweetly with a piece of Japanese candy, followed by hot, frothy green tea.

I came away feeling, as Soetsu Yanagi had described, quietly drawn into the beauty of the moment by being purified and made wholesome again. It was "*shibui* beauty, the beauty of the Tea ceremony, beauty that makes an artist of the viewer."

And it was a humbling moment, one that my meditation master Sri Chinmoy teaches as "True humility means giving joy to others," which Yamamoto had demonstrated.

How does this experience transfer at home? Start by enjoying quiet moments. First, it helps to clear away outer clutter on the table. Then take time to sip, and deeply inhale, from a warm cup of organic tea (whether green, black, or herbal). Close your eyes, let the moment suffuse you with its serenity, and drink deeply of it. Allow it to linger, from the tips of your fingers to the soles of your feet.

Whenever you feel the need for a moment of tranquility, reach into the inner pockets of your memories, pull forth this serene memory, and allow it to revitalize you again.

Purity in Design—Form Follows Function for Comfort and Utility

In 1960, editor Elizabeth Gordon introduced readers of *House Beautiful* to Japanese-style elegance by commenting, "*Shibui* is organic simplicity producing richness. It is not denial and austerity, for it is developed to the hilt.

"Rather, it is mastery and a sense of rightness (so they put the effort where it counts the most). This leads to exquisite perfection.[9] Consequently, being close to nature, it has nothing to do with abstractions."

As we have seen in the intervening years, Japanese designs have evolved due to artistic developments and consumer demands, and is a testimony to Soetsu Yanagi's

iteration, "for we are urged on in the search for truth (in beauty)."

Especially notable in the area of furniture design is the esteemed Japanese American wood maker George Nakashima. From his New Hope, Pennsylvania, home and studio, Nakashima fashioned stylish benches, cabinets, chairs, and tables. With his passing in 1990, his daughter Mira continues Nakashima's legacy of taking wood sculpture to greater heights of creativity and utility. For more information, visit www.nakashimawoodworker.com.

True artisans know that the painstaking and gratifying steps resulting in clean, simple lines are the result of love and careful attention to detail. Fashioned with a single-

[9] Gordon, "We Invite You to Enter a New Dimension: *Shibui*," *House Beautiful*, 95.

pointed focus, these dedicated efforts born of dynamic creative activity wordlessly beckon the observer. The overall feeling is one of deep serenity and satisfaction—in itself an exquisite manifestation of meditation in action—connecting artist with audience in their mutual appreciation of the fine arts.

We can tap into the examples shown in this book to enhance our homes and work environments by allowing comfort and utility for good design to facilitate function. We can begin, too, by letting go of old notions.

"The ideal of Greek beauty hardly permits of irregularity or asymmetry, for it was founded upon the symmetry of the human body. By contrast the Oriental found irregular beauty in nature outside the human form . . . the scientific thinking of Europe is founded in rational thought. In the East the foundation is in the heart and its inspiration, which to the Western mind, with its emphasis on the intellect, must appear very strange, for Eastern man jumps to his conclusions on wings of intuition, whereas Occidental man arrives at his by a steady progression of intellectual steps."[10] Soetsu Yanagi wrote this in 1954. Over half a century later, his advice is still relevant to free us of rational thought, to enable the grace of natural style to nourish and satisfy us from deep within our souls.

---

[10] Soetsu Yanagi, *The Unknown Craftsman*, 124.

4 ENDURING ELEMENTS OF JAPANESE DESIGN AND AESTHETICS

"One of the most important aspects of design is integration: not only the relationship of design to the process of manufacture, but to life itself and the creation of an environment."
— GEORGE NAKASHIMA

George Nakashima, born in Spokane, Washington, and woodworker extraordinaire, was also an architect with two degrees in the profession—the first from the University of Washington (1929) and a postgraduate degree from MIT (1930). Nakashima was the rare artist who balanced science and technology with soulful artistry.

"I'm very much interested in what constitutes creativity . . . because good things have to flow inwardly, in an integrated way. You find the nicest things in simplicity and directness," Nakashima said in a 1987 interview.[1]

But even earlier, Nakashima's theories on life, creativity, and design had been published in 1953 in the

---

[1] Mira Nakashima, *Nature Form & Spirit: The Life and Legacy of George Nakashima,* 119.

New York Times. "One of the most important aspects of design is integration: not only the relationship of design to the process of manufacture, but to life itself and the creation of an environment. Design is not a free-wheeling object in space but must relate to its conditions."[2]

Nakashima's lifelong passion for good design flowed from his inner realization that harmony was important for beauty to express divine truth. To achieve this balance of harmony in good design, he selected the appropriate materials and relevant instruments to craft his furniture designs. And although his innovative empathy allowed him the freedom to focus on the act of creation, it also entailed discipline on Nakashima's part to achieve a user-friendly appreciation for the items he crafted.[3]

This philosophy was deeply influenced by two years spent at the Sri Aurobindo Ashram in Pondicherry, India, where Nakashima supervised the building of Golconde, the ashram's dormitory. Golconde is on the American Institute of Architects Web site (www.aia.org) as the first, and one of the finest, enduring examples of International Modernism; it was completed in 1945.

Nakashima was one of Sri Aurobindo's first disciples. It was a very powerful experience as he considered himself a disciple of Sri Aurobindo's to the end of his days, his daughter, Mira, wrote.[4] On his thirty-third birthday, Nakashima received his spiritual name from Sri Aurobindo— Sundarananda, aptly meaning "one who delights in beauty."

[2] Ibid., 121.

[3] Ibid., 33.

[4] Ibid., 33. Mira herself was named after the ashram's mother, Mira Alfassa.

Mira wrote that her father designed all the furniture at Golconde as well, and that Nakashima even made Sri Aurobindo's bed with an adjustable backrest, "surely among the very earliest Nakashima furniture designs."[5]

"Not only was the design of Golconde unique, but the materials and construction itself are beautiful, 'like an Egyptian temple,'" Mira quoted the ashram's mother as saying. Although Golconde's basic design was by Antonin Raymond (he initially worked for Frank Lloyd Wright, rebuilding the Imperial Hotel in Tokyo, but soon struck out on his own), many creative decisions were made by Nakashima after Raymond returned to Japan.

Thus it happened that an American-born architect and wood artisan whose cultural heritage hailed from the Land of the Rising Sun (Japan) rediscovered his soul's heritage in the Land of Inner Consciousness (India). Tellingly, as a reflection of his integrated approach to balance and harmony in design, "So in work, as in living, Nakashima was a citizen of the world, a Hindu Catholic Shaker Japanese American," his daughter noted.

Pankaj Vir Gupta, AIA, and Christine Mueller from the University of Texas at Austin authored a 2005 case study on Golconde for an AIA Report on University Research. In a photo caption they noted: "The most striking feature of

---

[5] Ibid., 36.

Golconde is the skillful integration of the building with its landscape. The abstract permutations of the operable concrete skin are balanced with the serenity of the lotus pool and garden—a calm and meditative environment for devotees."

Another photo caption reads, "The north facing interior corridors facilitate a passive solar strategy for convection cooling. The sliding panels consist of staggered strips of teakwood, allowing for the passage of breezes, while maintaining visual privacy. Operable concrete louvers ensure constant air circulation between the north and south facades."

"Shifts in scale from structure to detail, and transitions between exterior and interior, occur with grace and precision. . . . The conceptual force of Golconde's design solution remains radical even by the standards of today (2005)," enthused Gupta and Mueller.[6]

Nakashima's intuitive proficiencies in organic architecture, as it were, stemmed from his Japanese sensibilities in naturally designing green, as well as deeper spiritual

---

[6] http://www.aia.org/SiteObjects/files/Gupta_color.pdf.

insights in respecting materials and terrain with compatible designs. Golconde's teak sliding panels and doors are similar to *fusuma* sliding paper panels, which enlarge or enclose interior spaces in Japan. The dormitory rooms allow cross ventilation without air-conditioning, and warm wood brings a rich patina to the sparse but neat interiors.

The spiritual precepts of Zen Buddhism in Japan have their roots in India, via China.[7] Perhaps it is not surprising to see it all come full circle in George Nakashima, gifted architect turned unparalleled wood artisan, who left architecture in 1942 to become, ever so humbly, a furniture designer and woodworker. "In treating inanimate objects with respect, a teahouse or a piece of Nakashima furniture becomes a place of humility, a direct experience, and purification; a way of finding one's center," Mira Nakashima noted.[8]

As an aside, my Indian spiritual master, Sri Chinmoy, was brought up at Sri Aurobindo's Ashram after he was orphaned at age eleven in 1942. Sri Chinmoy pays tribute to Japan with these words: "It is not nature's beauty in Japan—though that has its own value—but it is the inner beauty,

RIGHT: The Japanese tearoom space exudes an unmistakable warmth from the soothing patina of wood furnishings. (Photography by Carl Johansen.)

[7] Upon the Buddha's passing in the fifth century BCE in India, Buddhism reached China in the first century CE, Korea in the fourth century, and Japan in the sixth century, a process that took over a thousand years.

[8] Mira Nakashima, *Nature Form & Spirit: The Life and Legacy of George Nakashima*, 29.

inner softness, sweetness, tenderness, purity, and humility of Japan that have pleased God the Creator most powerfully."[9]

When John Fairman, owner of Honeychurch Antiques in Seattle, apprenticed to learn pottery-making from a well-known tea ceramicist, Seizan Takatori, he too learned the inner lessons of humility and nonattachment first before he was allowed to make progress with his outer efforts.

Sharing this anecdote in the catalogue for a March 2006 show in his gallery, *Layers & Legacies: Japanese Influences in Contemporary American Ceramics*, Fairman wrote: "For six months I made dozens of perfectly formed cups, each identical to the other, and at the end of those very long days, she would gleefully destroy each cup. After several months of anger, despair, and resentment, I finally found that I'd lost all attachment to everything that I made—and it was only then that Seizan stopped destroying my work.

"The making of each cup was slowly becoming an unconscious and meditative act, one in which I was merely a participant in the creation, rather than acting as the principal creator. This attitude of detachment extended to all aspects of kiln life, from digging clay and burning straw for ash glazes to the actual firing of the kiln itself.

"Nothing had changed in the four hundred years of making pottery at Seizan's kiln and nothing seemed to be as close to nature or as elemental."

For indeed, man at work is none other than a willing and ready instrument for the "Other Power" or "Higher Power" as Soetsu Yanagi called it, or Beauty and Truth, to manifest divinely, and as nature's unassuming landscape exemplifies so naturally. It was essential for the artist to learn nonattachment by letting go of ego and expectations

---

[9] Chinmoy, *Japan: Soul-Beauty's Heart-Garden*, 3.

to become a pure instrument of the divine, to ultimately find joy in his efforts, thereby gifting end users with satisfaction as well.

Long before sustainability, ergonomic design, and the notion of integral design in relating dwelling to landscape became buzzwords guiding architectural composition with (1) schematic design, (2) design development, and (3) resulting blueprints for construction today, Japan's designer-builders had been evolving their intuitive understanding of the forces of nature to building naturally with nature. As Tadao Ando reminds us, architecture has to remain mute to "let nature in the guise of sunlight and wind speak,"[10] to achieve exquisitely crafted structures and landscapes that endure through time, while silently blessing humanity with nature's serenity and joy.

---

[10] Or feng shui, as in the Chinese equivalent.

5   JAPANESE AESTHETICS AND AMERICAN SENSIBILITIES

"Individuals can transform a space, and hence make it particular, not by grand design but by the small celebrations of everyday life." — WITOLD RYBCZYNSKI

As the editor of *House Beautiful,* Elizabeth Gordon pointed out in 1960 (her observations still ringing true today) that we share many shelter instincts with the Japanese, and others around the world because everyone wants to live in a nurturing home environment. And, it's not about material splurging, either, in wanting to live a life of luxury and well-being.

In a survey by American Express Platinum published by *USA Today,* on the front page of its "Money Section B" on July 12, 2005, 770 households with incomes of $125,000 and over were asked, *"What is luxury?"* Forty-four percent of respondents chose happiness and satisfaction from being with family or friends and enjoying good times;

FACING: This meditation corner is highlighted by a naturally curving *tokobasira*. Shoes are verboten inside Japanese homes, especially on the *tatami* straw mat floor.

37 percent selected having enough time to do whatever you want and being able to afford it; and 19 percent opted for finer things in life that provide supreme comfort, beauty, and quality.

It's hardly surprising to learn of these responses. Confronted with today's intense lifestyle pace, we yearn for peaceful ways to relax and heal, and Japanese-style sensibilities offer refreshing alternatives to reenergize and rebalance our lives. Home is not merely a shell of a house. Our dwellings are imbued with our feelings and thoughts, with attempts at building and decorating and with using spaces that suit our activities. A home grows, along with its owners and residents, "not by grand design but by the small celebrations of everyday life," writes Witold Rybczynski in *The Most Beautiful House in the World*. This book is an engaging read of the author building his first house after becoming an architect, along with good insights into how homeowner dreams and designs on paper are translated into actual structures.[1]

So what goes into fashioning the most beautiful house in the world to suit our individual purposes? What "small celebrations of everyday life" can we create?

First, these celebrations of everyday life need to be as natural as can be in order to become good habits that motivate and inspire in the course of the daily grind. Second, they must be safe habits that enhance daily living. Third, they should be lovely to behold, constantly refreshing our moods by encouraging us to live in beauty and harmony.

[1] Rybczynski, 185.

Natural Style, Easy Grace

Simple celebrations of everyday life can be as easy as kicking off your shoes at the front door to symbolize leaving behind the harried outer world, then lighting incense and being soothed by the subtle aroma of lavender wafting through the house.

In 1665, a German visitor in a Dutch home observed that, "'In many houses, as in the holy places of the heathens, it is not permissible to ascend the stairs or set foot in a room without first removing one's shoes.' Jean-Nicholas de Parival, a French traveler, noticed the same thing, adding that, frequently, straw slippers were put on over one's shoes." In his first book, *Home: A Short History of An Idea*,[2] Rybczynski called this custom, "a desire to define the home as a separate, special place. . . . As every homemaker knows, the less furniture there is, the easier it is to keep a room clean, and this too may have had something to do with the relative sparseness of the Dutch interior, for these homes were spotlessly, immaculately, unbelievably clean."

For most Asian homes, removing shoes at the front door is a mark of respect to the house to honor its cleanliness and purity—by not trudging in outside dirt. At our home, after removing their shoes, guests are offered soft slippers to wear.

The benefits are many. Less dirt and small rocks gouge our wood floors, gently buffed by bare feet in the warmer seasons and by softly slippered feet in the cooler months. Bare feet are treated to the comforting sensation of walking on smooth wood, an uncommon experience in itself. Less time is spent cleaning the floor. Infants and young children with more sensitive immune systems inhale

[2] Rybczynski, 64–66.

BELOW: It's a luxury to go barefoot in a Japanese-style room at Golden Door spa, adorned with a *tokonoma* alcove, or sacred shrine in honor of natural beauty. (Courtesy of Golden Door, Escondido, California.)

cleaner indoor air, and the floor is not a toxic playpen covered with less visible pollutants "shoe-ed in" from the streets.

The same practice prevails in Japanese homes. Shoes are left in the *genkan*, or foyer, and traded for house slippers, with the gesture being both symbolic and a conscious desire to leave behind the outer world by shedding, literally, the first obvious steps—shoes.

Japanese homes are also unbelievably immaculate, which adds to the feeling of purity—and one that's enhanced by burning incense. In fact, the Japanese honor "the way of incense," *koh-do* (*koh* for "incense," *do* for "the way"), by acknowledging the olfactory senses as a necessary aesthetic contributing to an overall pleasant home ambiance.

Since the Muromachi era (1333–1573), the Japanese have embraced the "Ten Virtues of *Koh*," the practice of incense appreciation that discreetly removes malodorous odors and purifies the air, indoors and out. According to the Japanese company Nippon Kodo, which started making incense for the emperor over 400 years ago, burning quality incense

transports the senses to a meditative realm while comforting and inspiring the aesthete.[3]

At the end of the workday, eagerly looking forward to returning home to *the* ultimate sanctuary that sustains us with its many comforting touches is truly joyful anticipation.

Soak in some quiet time. Ask what brings you joy from the depths of your soul. Be confident with whatever inspires from deep within. For the Japanese, it's removing shoes to symbolize a return to home as sanctuary. Olfactory purification with *koh-do* (or any form of aromatherapy) promotes a sweet-smelling consciousness that uplifts the senses. Play with different ideas, and imbue your home with delightful new ways to revitalize your energy.

Going with the Green

Japan's population is about one-half the population of the United States but is thirty times smaller in area. Japan's natural resources are not as abundant, either. But what the Japanese do possess is ingenuity and creativity doubtlessly brought on by force of necessity. An enduring and endearing Japanese cultural trait is a frugality that is not stingy, but one that is respectful of scarce resources and makes the most of what's available.

[3] http://www.nipponkodo.com/culture/index.html.

That's what happened in an earlier time in the United States too. As the saying goes, Rome was not built in a day. It's building on materials available now that results in satisfaction later on down the road. Rybczynski reported in *The Most Beautiful House in the World,* "The first structure completed by Thomas Jefferson at Monticello was a tiny one-room cottage—about two hundred square feet in area—which he occupied for four and a half years, first as a bachelor and later as a married man, until the main house was complete."[4]

And that's why Japan has a long history of building green while saving bundles of greenbacks. For going green is simply intuition and common sense at work with scarce natural resources. Inevitably, simplicity begets luxury with sustainable results that benefit both humanity and the environment.

The photos in this section share some green methods Japanese homeowners have traditionally employed to catch rainwater for watering the landscape, cool indoor areas passively, optimize space use, and capture natural light.

[4] Rybczynski, 137.

Beauty, or God, Is in the Details

The luxury of incorporating aesthetic details into home and garden can be as simple as a fresh coat of paint that pleases, or rearranging furniture to maximize room space and easy flow.

For the Japanese, beauty is "not grand scale nor imposing mass, but gracefulness and refinement in an architectural composition. A refined beauty in limited mass and space was [and is the] first and final aim"; this "endless pursuit of elegance" has resulted in the "designer's practiced sense of beauty," Hirotaro Ota summarized in compiling *Japanese Architecture and Gardens*.[5]

Additionally, images in this section show the intricate craftsmanship of Japanese artistry. Quality workmanship is always of paramount consideration in Japanese construction.

---

[5] Ota, 23.

BELOW: The natural artistry of Japanese design is reflected in the preponderant use of wood as a building material. Alcove details show off the wood's natural grain and beauty, especially the *tokobasira* (the integral post, seen here separating the built-in couch from the dresser).

And as breathtaking as Japanese design is, its principles are relevant and reasonably easy to emulate today. "The effect of fine materials, the logic of construction, and beautiful proportions, is a genuine architectural beauty in accordance with the ideals of Modern architecture," Ota suggested.[6]

It takes a keen eye, plus taking the time and doing the extra work, to hone any skill. In the process, what may seem to be an indulgence surfaces as pure devotion to appreciating beauty with practical applications, an indulgence for many to enjoy. Isn't the goal of being happy similar to enjoying the small celebrations of life, surrounded by comfort and beauty?

In fact, "The Japanese people's innate feeling for beauty and the high importance they attach to work are characteristics that have continued virtually unchanged from the pre-industrial to the industrial age, and many of the industrialized products of modern Japan possess these age-old virtues in modern form," Mitsukuni Yoshida commented in his essay on "Japanese Aesthetic Ideals," in the 1980 exhibition catalogue for *Japan Style,* at the Victoria and Albert Museum in London.[7]

---

[6] Ibid., 29.
[7] Yoshida, 22.

6 LIVING WITH NATURAL GRACE, IN THE JAPANESE STYLE

"By the mid 1930's Frank Lloyd Wright's architectural art was fully developed. It was organic, and the precedent was Farther Asia; yet it no longer depended upon the outward appearance of Japanese buildings. Organic architecture, Wright had come to realize, was traceable back to a venerable figure of the Chou Dynasty in China . . . 'Although I did not know it then, the principle now at the center of our modern movement was very clearly stated as early as five hundred years before Christ by the Chinese philosopher Lao Tze . . . that the reality of the building consisted not in four walls and a roof but inhered in the space within, the space to be lived in.' (wrote Wright)" — CLAY LANCASTER [1]

What does it take to build in tune with nature, to achieve that artless naturalness prompting Frank Lloyd Wright to enthuse in using nature's metaphors, "bird-like" and "turtle-like," in describing Japanese houses a century ago?

Hirotaro Ota, editor of *Japanese Architecture and Gardens*, wrote, "For the Japanese, a building does not resist or subdue nature. While it is built by man, it is no more than

---

[1] Lancaster, *The Japanese Influence in America*, 159–60.

UPPER: A lower *koetsu-gaki* lattice fence keeps pets along the pathway and out of the flower garden. The curved fence (*gaki*) aligns with the path's curvature, built from a copper armature inside and hidden by bamboo on the exterior. (Courtesy of Bamboo Fencer, Inc.)
LOWER: Nature's peaceful beauty suffuses a Japanese strolling garden at Golden Door spa. (Courtesy of Golden Door, Escondido, California.)

a part of the whole view of nature as if it were a tree in the landscape."[2]

In this country, the trek to building naturally has left its tracks in a 1977 publication, *A Pattern Language*.[3] Two hundred fifty design suggestions by architects and architectural students at the Center for Environmental Structure in Berkeley, California, aimed to help homeowners not trained as architects incorporate human patterns of behavior into designing spaces that would resonate with utility and vitality.

[2] Ota, 23.
[3] Christopher Alexander, Sara Ishikawa, and Murray Silverstein, New York City: Oxford University Press.

"One thing that was new to me in creating a Japanese-inspired garden was using many colors and textures of leaves, from light gray green to dark red, rather than using flowers for color. The contrast adds depth and interest to the landscape, and the use of evergreens adds a timeless quality that is calming."

— SAKINA VON BRIESEN, Chief Administrator, Chado New Mexico

Twenty-five years later, two of the authors have edited down these 250 initial suggestions to ten basic concepts for crafting the well-lived-in home. Max Jacobson and Murray Silverstein, with their architectural partner Barbara Winslow, published *Patterns of Home: The Ten Essentials of Enduring Design* in 2002, filled with useful ideas of site integration, material selection, and other design details.

Americans are learning to listen—to the heart's intuition for smarter spatial use and flow, and incorporating cost-effective green building techniques in harmony with nature. We're starting to integrate the garden courtyard (as the Japanese and Chinese have been doing for centuries) and other outdoor spaces as extensions of interior spaces to optimize functionality at home and at work.

The following Japanese garden and teahouse examples are but two suggestions to enhance our affinity for retrieving travel memories that also revive. Entertaining at home with an appreciation of Nature's ever-changing Beauty can be as simple as sipping tea in an oasis of serenity—in our very own tea garden (*chaniwa*) and tearoom.[4]

The Japanese Garden

"The Japanese garden rearranges the natural landscape in order to create a new beauty from nature," architect Hirotaro Ota advised, in explaining Wright's incredulous exclamations on the naturalness of organic architecture in Japan. How do the Japanese do it?

Invariably, they consult the first recorded resource on designing Japanese gardens, *Sakuteiki*, by the aristocrat Tachibana no Toshitsuna (1028–1094).[5] "The very first

---

[4] In their book, *Introduction to Japanese Architecture*, David and Michiko Young describe the Japanese teahouse as composed of the building itself and the garden, page 63.

[5] Jiro Takei and Marc P. Keane translated an updated version of *Sakuteiki: Visions of the Japanese Garden* in 2001.

". . . the beauty of nature is the expression of the One who is all Beauty. Whenever we see something, we see inside that thing the inner presence, the inner consciousness, of its creator. The Creator of nature is God Himself. He expresses Himself in and through Nature. When we see nature's beauty, we get overwhelming joy because the Creator and Owner is God. When we see a house, if we love the owner, we love the possession. The One who is all Beauty is inside His creation, like a mother's heart is inside her child. A mother's heart cannot be separated from the child's existence." — S R I C H I N M O Y , *A Galaxy of Beauty's Stars*, at http://www.srichinmoylibrary.com/galaxy-beauty-stars/22.html

instruction in the eleventh-century *Sakuteiki*[6] (*Treatise on Garden-Making*) is to observe and learn from nature. The idea is not simply to transpose a view that you have seen—that is merely imagination—but to absorb the atmosphere and feeling, and to use your own ideas and imagination to re-create the same mood in your garden," wrote landscape architect Takashi Sawano (who has relocated to London) in the very first sentence of his book, *Creating Your Own Japanese Garden*.

David Slawson, in his essay "Authenticity in Japanese Landscape Design," echoes this centuries-old advice to heed "from within—from the desires and culture of those who will use the garden, from the site and its surroundings (including the regional landscape), and from locally available materials."[7]

---

[6] Sawano spelled it *Sakiteiki* in his book.

[7] Jonas, *Japanese-Inspired Gardens*, 10.

BAMBOO

Q: How can a bamboo floor be maintained, and how can quality bamboo be chosen?

A: Obviously, a good finish kept clean is important. Shoes, soles, and bare feet do not damage a bamboo floor; grit does. The absolute most important parameter in bamboo's durability is its harvesting time—more important than species of bamboo, finish, total age, and environment. The time from the first shoots to harvest should not be less than three years.

Q: How can bamboo left outside be repaired?

A: The natural wax on the bamboo provides protection from sun and rain (and, hence, rot). However, the natural coating will oxidize, particularly when subject to UV from the sun's rays, and turn a silvery gray. If the oxidized parts are left on uncleaned, it will get a flaky, whitish, unattractive look. Polishing with heat, soap, and, often, bleach leaves a smooth coat of wax that does not flake off. Oil-based sealers can be applied to the waxy bamboo, but this coating will scratch off until it has hardened—which can take months. Minor scratches are invisible if you use a clear oil-based protective coating. I find Cabot's Australian Hardwood Timber Oil excellent, although the Cabot's people will tell you it will not work on bamboo, as they want the oil to penetrate— which it will not do unless you let the wax weather away. I find the wax and oils blend pretty well, and in a few months, the treated bamboo becomes scratch resistant. Once weathered, you can wash it, apply a deck sealer, and it will be well protected. If you wait until the deck sealer penetrates (when wax is weathered away), the final color will be darker even if you use a clear sealer. Bamboo stuck in the ground will last six years before rotting away in most soil conditions.

— *From Dave Flanagan, owner, Bamboo Fencer, Inc.*

The bibliography for this book has a category on Japanese gardens. Too in-depth and diverse for the short section here, these titles are highly informative on various types of Japanese gardens. They cover the dry garden variety known as *karesansui*—of sand, pebbles, and stones simulating a winding river, moss, and minimal plantings; tea gardens (*chaniwa*); strolling gardens; and others.

Tearooms and Teahouses for Entertaining with Tranquility

No book on Japanese style is complete without a passing mention of that hallowed Japanese custom now enjoyed the world over, and which was imported from China—tea drinking. But like all other foreign ideas that caught their fancy, the Japanese gave it their own special touch that resulted in *Chado*, or the Way of Tea.

Originally, tea drinking was employed by Buddhist monks as a tactic to stay awake during meditation. But the great tea master Sen no Rikyu (1522–1591) elevated its status to a rarified level, from which developed *chanoyu*, the

tea ceremony. A delightful description of *chanoyu*'s aesthetic philosophy and practices according to Grand Tea Master Dr. Soshitsu Sen XV is available online at the following Web site: http://www.holymtn.com/tea/TeaLifeZenTea.htm. Many similar sources are also online.

It was serendipitous meeting Chado New Mexico's chief administrator and Urasenke Tankokai–certified *Chado* instructor Sakina von Briesen at the end of my research. She offered these insights for building a tearoom: "There are myriad design considerations for tearooms. Primarily, one wants guests, upon entering a tea space (it doesn't have to be a formal tearoom), to have a sense of having crossed a threshold into another world.

"The world of *chanoyu* reflects the four principles of tea— *wa kei sei jaku* (harmony, respect, purity, and tranquility)—in the spatial proportions of the tearoom, choice of materials, cleanliness, muted colors, soft lighting, and overall atmosphere.

"Since many of life's distractions are excluded from a tea space, it makes it possible for the host and guests to be fully present together. You want your guests to feel calm, but not fall asleep. The design and proportions of a tea space are asymmetrical, and are meant to awaken one's spirit to a new appreciation of beauty. Often, with that heightened awareness comes a feeling of gratitude.

"The tearoom can be a modern or traditional aesthetic and still create this feeling of freshness in the guests. It is very important, though, that the room functions well as a good space for making, and sharing, tea—which takes practice and experience with *chanoyu* on the part of the host-designer," von Briesen suggested.

The von Briesens had just finished converting a spare bedroom into a tearoom, and had built a tea shelter (where guests wait until they are called to *chanoyu*) in their garden. The following photos show the couple's painstaking efforts with attention to detail in building the two tea spaces and a peaceful Japanese tea garden (*chaniwa*) in their backyard.

Before long, Sakina invited me to a very special *chanoyu*. Her husband, Hans, carefully explained each gesture and movement. Chado New Mexico's flyer shares this pearl: "Served with a respectful heart and received with gratitude, a bowl of Tea satisfies both the physical and spiritual thirst." My cup runneth over, as memories revive, of this heartfelt gift of *chanoyu*.

Each *chanoyu* is indeed a once-in-a-lifetime shared experience between guests and host, immortalized in the expression *ichi-go ichi-e*, "each meeting only once," given the transcendent highlights of each passing moment shared among friends—and as graceful as Nature's ephemeral environs.

7 CROSS-CULTURAL EXAMPLES IN AMERICA

"Our challenge at Ten Thousand Waves is to build with natural materials, yet be true to the Japanese aesthetic. We try to use authentic materials whenever possible, such as bamboo. But it's mainly working out details that convey a sense of authenticity while using local materials and building with site requirements in mind."

—DUKE KLAUCK, owner of Ten Thousand Waves

Santa Feans and visitors are lucky to indulge in the only Japanese-style *sento*, or public-bath-cum-health-spa, in this country—Ten Thousand Waves. Snuggly nestled against a hilly terrain three miles north of town, the waters bubble up from a fractured limestone aquifer 900 feet below ground level—all the more remarkable in a high-desert location experiencing drought.

Ten Thousand Waves celebrated its silver anniversary in 2006. It is a tribute to its founder, Duke Klauck, who had the vision to develop and build Japanese style in a predominantly arid southwestern mountain desert over 7,000 feet above sea level.

FACING: Elemental design components of wood, stone, reed, and translucent *shoji* (screens of handmade paper) quietly harmonize in the courtyard.

"The site was the only available land near Santa Fe that was unzoned then, a one-mile stretch of Hyde Park Road between city limits and the national forest. It was rural enough to be beautiful and quiet, and close enough to town for a quick trip," said Klauck.

Today, the Waves also provides lodging in twelve guest houses, with more planned. Additional treatment rooms are being built, and a restaurant featuring *izakaya* finger food (or tapas-style food) and a bar will be up and running in 2008.

"It's hard to strictly follow the rules of Japanese building here in New Mexico, given the different materials we have," said Jon Driscoll, head builder at the Waves. Driscoll had been a student of Shintoism and became a Buddhist priest while living in San Francisco. He was invited to study with his *sensei* (master) in Japan for five years, during which time he honed his Japanese building skills.

Driscoll has been building at the Waves since 2002. Photos of the Waves are interspersed with shots from Japan taken by Deborah Fleig, Klauck's girlfriend. Klauck draws his design inspirations from frequent trips to Japan. Driscoll, with his customary inventiveness, then builds on Klauck's ideas.

LEFT: The reception counter at Ten Thousand Waves has Japanese design motifs carved in wood.

In fact, Japanese guests to the Waves marvel at this oasis resembling an *onsen,* or hot springs, on the high desert, and comment on the authentic adaptations that Klauck and Driscoll present together with their builders. They share some of their ideas here, with photo captions explaining how these local adaptations came about.

Golden Door in Escondido, California, is another spa built with Japanese designs and accents. The original owner, Deborah Szekely (founder of the first modern spa in 1940 with her late husband, Edmond) envisioned Golden Door as a *honjin.* Forty lucky women guests stay in this destination spa for a week, vigorously adhering to an

RIGHT: A carved *ranma*, or transom, softens natural light diffusing into a treatment room at Ten Thousand Waves.

exercise program in the mornings and duly being pampered in the afternoons with facials, bodywork, and massages. A few weeks in the year are open to men only.

During the Edo period (1600–1868) the *honjin* inn was officially designated for Japanese aristocrats and their retainers, high-ranking priests, and other high officials. *Waki-honjin* inns catered to the lower ranks, while *hatagoya* inns served the ordinary people during this feudal period in Japan's history.[1]

As these garden and landscape photos show, a little imagination can set up some exotic experiences at home.

[1] Young, *Introduction to Japanese Architecture*, 76.

LEFT: A *torii*, or gateway, to the Japanese abode or temple is usually painted a bright vermilion red, providing a striking contrast to the natural surroundings. Note the two different roof ridgepoles, each capped with a different *monsho*, or crest. (Courtesy of Ten Thousand Waves. Photography by Deborah Fleig.)

BELOW: A contemporary take on the traditional Japanese front door builds on a stylized, recessed exterior. The smaller door within the main door to the lower left is a rendition of the Japanese teahouse door (*nijiriguchi*), lowered to symbolize guests' humility upon entering a sacred space for the meditative tea ceremony. (Courtesy of Ten Thousand Waves. Photography by Deborah Fleig.)

FACING ABOVE: A Japanese *torii*, or gate, with thatched roof anchors the simple fence made of bamboo posts and transverse supports of split bamboo. (Courtesy of Ten Thousand Waves. Photography by Deborah Fleig.)

FACING BELOW: The Japanese aesthetic is one of cleanliness, orderliness, and safety for all. Many smaller streets are pedestrian only, providing for safe travel. (Courtesy of Ten Thousand Waves. Photography by Deborah Fleig.)

FACING: Foliage varying from silvery-gray greens to rich dark greens conveys a quiet serenity to the overall landscape at Golden Door spa. (Courtesy of Golden Door, Escondido, California.)

BELOW LEFT: Brown bark, green pine needles, a *toro* (stone lantern), and a boulder on a green lawn invite the contemplation of nature. The green moss on the *toro* is a prized natural embellishment. (Courtesy of Golden Door, Escondido, California.)

BELOW RIGHT: A miniature Shinto shrine along a garden path pays homage to the *kami*, or spirits, of nature. (Courtesy of Ten Thousand Waves. Photography by Deborah Fleig.)

RIGHT: Boulders shore up an embankment along a garden wall. (Courtesy of Ten Thousand Waves. Photography by Deborah Fleig.)

FACING: Water gently flows into a *tsukabai*, or garden water basin, and cools off a high-desert xeriscaped garden. (Courtesy of Stone Forest.)

BELOW LEFT: Handwoven hemp curtains typically front Japanese businesses, providing textural contrasts to the rough concrete wall and colorful paper lanterns. (Courtesy of Ten Thousand Waves. Photography by Deborah Fleig.)

BELOW RIGHT: Folded white strips of paper are New Year flags signifying good luck—pure and true. (Courtesy of Ten Thousand Waves. Photography by Deborah Fleig.)

RIGHT: Embedded in a corner of the garden is a *tanuki*, a symbol of good luck for businesses. *Tanukis* are raccoon-like, synonymous with the Native American trickster animal, the coyote—beguiling and wily in attracting attention. (Courtesy of Ten Thousand Waves. Photography by Deborah Fleig.)

8 A YEN FOR GOOD DESIGN

"Noren are ungathered split curtains made of cloth or hemp. . . . Since it flutters in the breeze, the noren enables one to 'see' the wind, and, when used in conjunction with wind chimes that enable one to 'hear' the wind, it is really as though one is 'experiencing' the wind." — K O J I   Y A G I

Perhaps no other Japanese-style design and how-to book has had a bigger impact on American do-it-yourselfers or home builders than architect Koji Yagi's *A Japanese Touch for Your Home.*

Insightful and sprinkled with dashes of the accomplished architect's erudite eye for design, the Japanese yen to honor details, and the poet's lyrical style, Yagi's book is a treasury filled with informative architectural line drawings, illustrations, and breathtaking photography in both color and black and white.

"Closeness to nature is the ultimate goal of Japanese architecture," Yagi affirmed. As we have acknowledged

FACING: This room (and entire home) designed by Aaron Bohrer gracefully adapts Japanese post-and-beam construction and furnishings to contemporary living. (Photography by Robert Reck.)

in previous chapters, and as Yagi reiterates, the Japanese perception of beauty is "seen in the concepts of *wabi* (simple quietude) and *sabi* (elegant simplicity). . . . At the same time it contains aspects of the philosophy of 'less is more' . . . of enclosing a simple structure with a thin membrane to create a composition in which there is a sense of tension in simplicity."[1]

This "sense of tension in simplicity" invites the home designer to consider site-specific requirements and to use local materials whenever possible to benefit both inhabitants and environment.

Innovative Adaptations Satisfy across Cultures

Not coincidentally, American artisans such as Michael Zimber heed similar preferences for crafting world-class pieces from natural materials for interior and exterior spaces that are beautiful and functional. What is Zimber's appeal for architects, interior designers, and homeowners to visit Stone Forest, his Santa Fe, New Mexico, showroom, since 1989? "Less is more. Simple beauty. Emphasize natural materials—the stone, copper, bronze, or wood should always speak louder than the design," Zimber answered unequivocally.[2]

[1] Yagi, 8.
[2] www.stoneforest.com.

"Japan's childlike flower consciousness—a beautiful flower—is reaching the highest in terms of beauty and purity. As soon as I think of Japan, my mind feels beauty, my heart feels purity, and my life feels humility."

— S R I   C H I N M O Y , *Japan: Soul-Beauty's Heart-Garden*

When asked why we fall for "less is more" and "simple beauty," Zimber explained, "Life is hectic and crazy. Many Americans crave soul-healing calm. Instinctively and experientially, we know that the natural world holds the cure. Part of the Japanese aesthetic is the idea of distilling the essence of nature and bringing it into the home and garden, and our designs strive to achieve this."

Zimber started his business after ten years of "living in the wilds of the world and making a living as a climbing, kayaking, and ski guide. When I decided it was time to grow up, I drew on my experiences in the outdoors, combining my love of wilderness with stone carving and learning about Japanese gardening."

Then, Zimber pondered how he could combine his love of nature and her beauty into a workable scenario. "Having felt Nature's expansion and peace, I wanted to somehow bottle up that essence and bring it home to enjoy. That's how I started experimenting and interpreting the Japanese aesthetic—to the world of fountains and contemporary art. That was how Stone Forest developed," Zimber said.

Stone Forest's best-sellers are their edgy yet restrained and Zen-like contemporary free-style fountains for outdoors and indoors. With today's growing cocooning instincts to relax at home, bathtubs are also selling very well. Italian marble bathtubs made at their local workshop—of Carrara, Perlato Svevo, and Crema Marfil marble—command prices upwards of $16,000, at press time.

Meanwhile, bamboo artisan Dave Flanagan in Ashland, Massachusetts, was also influenced by the Japanese aesthetic in using natural materials for building purposes. In describing his fondness for working with the material, Flanagan said, "Bamboo is a marvel of good engineering that I respect. It places material in exactly the correct place, and in the correct amount, to provide great strength in compression, tension, and in resisting buckling. It is clean and pleasant to the touch and eye."

Flanagan said his best-seller, "the classic *Kenninji-gaki*, is extremely popular and a great relief from the standard American stockade fence." His Web site lists different designs, as well as good background information on working with, and caring for, bamboo.[3]

Like many receptive souls with an affinity for working with nature, and a willing participant in serendipity, Flanagan described how he got started. "I was sent to Panama by the coast guard in my last tour of duty. We were surrounded by beautiful large bamboo in a variety of species. My wife

---

[3] www.bamboofencer.com.

and I became distressed by the damage done to tropical forests, the loss of habitat, and ugly loss of income for the natives when timber was harvested for short-term gain.

"But bamboo does have the ability to grow and spread in these barren areas and reclaim its habitat, sequester carbon, hold land, and grow topsoil—plus providing a useful product that, like all grasses, withstands periodic harvesting without damaging the plant. After thirty-four years in the coast guard, I retired and started the company. The goal of providing an alternative to hardwoods, income for the indigenous people, and reclaiming abused forests is being realized at least in part through our close relationship with Yucatan Bamboo," Flanagan pointed out.

With almost two decades of crafting fine bamboo arts

for the home, Flanagan is heartened by "more Americans traveling to Japan and seeing how bamboo is used in places like Kyoto—with respect, great care, and class. Other Americans are interested in renewable materials and have discovered bamboo's great strength and rapid growth through the green movement."

Flanagan and Zimber are both well traveled and love the outdoors. For two decades, two men living in different parts of the country (in the northeast and in the southwest), and working with very different natural materials, have successfully transitioned to design professions that transcend cultural boundaries—in instinctively satisfying American tastes with relevant renditions of the Japanese aesthetic.

LEFT: Japanese-style adaptations of design details in this room at Ten Thousand Waves range from acrylic *shoji* to the whimsical wall sconce. (Photography by Kim Kurian.)

The Art of Life

It is appropriate to conclude with observations on Fumihiko Maki, one of three Japanese Pritzker Laureates, who received the Pritzker Architecture Prize in 1993. Maki spent ten years teaching and working in the United States before returning home to practice in Tokyo. He obtained his Master of Architecture degree from Harvard's Graduate School of Design in 1956, and taught there as well from 1962 to 1965.

From the Pritzker Web site, Maki is honored as "a student of two cultures whose fusion of the two influences has been greatly acclaimed . . . he likens his Tokyo to Manhattan, where dynamic and static elements are in continual conflict, and being in its midst is like standing on the beach as waves ceaselessly advance and recede."

"Maki worked at, or observed, numerous offices in Japan and other countries. One of the conclusions he drew was that an office, and by extension, design itself, is a matter of individual character, and that an office is itself a work of art," noted the Pritzker site.[4]

And indeed, design is a powerful reflection of humanity's eternal quest of living Life and its myriad manifestations as a beautiful art form—be it Japanese, American, or otherwise.

---

[4] www.pritzkerprize.com.

An array of *wabi sabi* elements on the right is an engaging visual counterpoint to the formal display on the left for this wall display. (Photography by Carl Johansen.)

HISTORICAL PERIODS OF JAPAN

1989–present	Heisei
1926–1989	Showa
1912–1926	Taisho, increased assimilation of western technology and the arts
1868–1912	Meiji, Japan opened up to Commodore Perry and the world
1600–1868	Edo or Tokugawa, a prosperous and insulated era that introduced "fusion style" *sukiya*, or teahouse, architecture that allowed owners the freedom to combine *shoin* and *sukiya* design styles; saw the appearance of *ukiyo-e*, or "floating world" woodblock prints
1573–1600	Momoyama, civil strife and rise of the merchant class
1333–1573	Muromachi, the emergence of *shoin* (developed from an abbot's study or "book room") style of formal audience hall with *tokonoma* to display art treasures from China and Korea, plus the introduction of the rustic (*wabi*) teahouse as "a counter aesthetic to the palatial, refined audience hall,"[1] where samurais purified their spirit with *Chado* before, and after, going to war

1185–1333	Kamakura, *Chado* ("the Way of Tea"[2]) introduced from China by the returning monk Eisen, who founded the Zen sect in 1191
794–1185	Heian, Japanese garden artistry was well developed at this time,[3] celebrated by symbols drawn from nature's grace and elegance
710–794	Nara
645–710	Hakuho
538–645	Asuka, the arrival of Buddhism from China around 552
300–710	Tomb Mound (with overlaps)
250 BCE–300 CE	Yayoi
15,000–250 BCE	Jomon

[1] From Matthew Welch's informative Q&A on the Web site of the Minneapolis Institute of the Arts: http://www.artsmia.org/art-of-asia/architecture/japanese-teahouse-interview.cfm.
[2] Urasenke Foundation's Web site is information packed: http://www.urasenke.org/tradition/index.php.
[3] Addiss, *Traditional Japanese Arts and Culture*, 58.

G L O S S A R Y

andon	Floor lamp with a *washi* (handmade paper) lampshade
byobu	Movable folding screens to delineate room space or to block drafts
Chado	The Way of Tea
chanoyu	Tea ceremony—art of tea meditation among friends, to purify the senses
chigadana	Staggered, asymmetrical display shelves
engawa	Veranda or porch that opens up as extra living space in the summer, while providing extra insulation when closed in the winter
furo	Bathtub constructed from *hinoki*, a fragrant Japanese cypress, with water traditionally warmed by a brazier
furoshiki	The art of wrapping items with a piece of fabric—from carrying five eggs home from market to a *bento* (lunch box)
fusuma	Light, sliding, papered doors that enlarge or divide room spaces
genkan	Entrance or foyer
goza	Thinner floor mats that roll up
hibachi	Brazier for cooking and heating

hisaku	Bamboo dipper
ikebana	School of floral arrangement that emphasizes using flowers, branches, and greens in graceful harmony with the seasons
irori	Sunken, open hearth in the living room for cooking and heating
kakejiku	Hanging scroll, and the only item in the tearoom that guests bow to (apart from each other) in honoring the sacred wisdom it invokes for *chanoyu*
karesansui	Dry garden consisting of rocks, pebbles simulating a winding river, raked sand, and perhaps some moss
kasuri	Hand-dyed, indigo and white cloth for clothing, *noren*, and other uses
koh	Incense; *koh-do* is the Japanese art of incense appreciation
machiai	Tea shelter where guests await the host's invitation to the tea ceremony
mingei	Folk art, literally "the people's art," coined by the aesthete Soetsu Yanagi
monsho	Family crests, typically stylized round icons as shown in the opening pages to this book's sections

nijiriguchi	The low teahouse entrance through which guests crawl to enter, as a symbol of humility and gratitude for participating in Chado.
noren	Curtain with free-floating panels hung across the top of doorways
onsen	Hot springs, or health spas, that cleanse the body and purify the spirit
roji	Path of stepping-stones, or poetically "the dewy path," that gets hosed down with water to welcome guests en route to the teahouse
shakkei	The art of using outside scenery as a backdrop to complement the interior
shikki	Lacquer-ware
shinden	Aristocratic residential enclaves and mansions of the wealthy
sento	Japanese public baths
shoin	The abbot's study or book room in monasteries that became fashionable architecture during the Muromachi period
shoji	Translucent paper panel made from *washi*
sudare	Rolled blinds made from split bamboo or reeds
sukiya	A teahouse, built with precision joinery sans hardware
tansu	Heavy storage cabinets; *mizuya tansu* is a kitchen cabinet; *kaidan tansu* is a chest with steps that also acts as a stairway
tatami	Tightly woven floor mat of straw and reed, 3 by 6 feet, and 2 1/4 inches thick; traditionally, rooms were measured by *tatami* size, and a standard tearoom size (*yojohan*) is a 4 1/2 *tatami* mat room, about 9 square feet
tokobasura	The defining post at the sacred alcove that honors the owner's personality
tokonoma	The sacred alcove, or "treasure room," that showcases refined restraint—a scroll invoking a celebration mood and a seasonal floral arrangement
torii	An impressive temple gateway with no doors
toro	Stone lantern, subtly amplifying garden shadows when lit with votives
tsuitate	A mobile room divider carved from wood; may include a shoji panel
tsukabai	A hollowed-out rock basin containing fresh water for tea ceremony guests to ritually cleanse their mouths and hands before entering the teahouse
ukiyo-e	Woodblock prints of the "floating world," euphemism for dalliances with courtesans
washi	Handmade paper (preferably hand-torn, rather than cut with scissors)
zabuton	Large floor cushion

FACING: This is a contemporary take on a Japanese-style bath. The bather typically scrubs and showers off first, before settling into a relaxing and salubrious soak in the bathtub.

BIBLIOGRAPHY

Japanese Aesthetics and Design

Addiss, Stephen, Gerald Groemer, and J. Thomas Rimer, eds. *Traditional Japanese Arts and Culture.* Honolulu: University of Hawai'i Press, 2006.

Arsdale, Jay Van. *Shoji: How to Design, Build, and Install Japanese Screens.* Tokyo: Kodansha International, 1988.

Asensio, Paco, ed. *Le Corbusier.* New York: teNeues Publishing Company, 2003.

Bornoff, Nicholas, and Michael Freeman. *Things Japanese.* New Clarendon, VT: Tuttle, 2002.

Carpenter, Juliet Winters, and Sen Soshitsu. *Seeing Kyoto.* Tokyo: Kodansha International, 2005.

Chinmoy, Sri. *Japan: Soul-Beauty's Heart-Garden.* New York: Agni Press, 1993.

Conran, Terence. *The Ultimate House Book for Home Design in the Twenty-First Century.* London: Conran Octopus Limited, 2003.

De Waal, Edmund, ed. *Timeless Beauty: Traditional Japanese Art from the Montgomery Collection.* Milan: Skira editore, 2002.

Dunn, Michael. *Inspired Design: Japan's Traditional Arts.* Milan: 5 Continents, 2005.

Ekiguchi, Kunio, and Ruth S. McCreery. *Japanese Crafts and Customs.* Tokyo: Kodansha International, Ltd., 1987.

Ekuan, Kenji. *The Aesthetics of the Japanese Lunchbox.* Translated by Don Kenny. Cambridge, MA: The MIT Press, 1998.

Engel, Heino. *Measure and Construction of the Japanese House.* North Clarendon, VT: Tuttle, 2000.

Freeman, Michael. *Space: Japanese Design Solutions for Compact Living.* New York: Universe Publishing, 2004.

Freeman, Michael, and Michiko Rico Nose. *Japan Modern: New Ideas for Contemporary Living.* North Clarendon, VT: Periplus/Tuttle, 2000.

Futagawa, Yukio. *Traditional Japanese Houses.* New York: Rizzoli, 1983.

Heinrich, Engel. *The Japanese House: A Tradition for Contemporary Architecture.* North Clarendon, VT: Tuttle, 1964.

Henrichsen, Christoph, and Roland Bauer. *Japan—Culture of Wood: Buildings, Objects, Techniques.* Basel: Birkhauser, 2004.

Hibi, Sadao. *Japanese Tradition in Color and Form: Architecture.* Tokyo: Graphic-sha Publishing, 1987.

Hibi, Sadao, Motoji Niwa, and Jay W. Thomas. *Snow, Wave, Pine: Traditional Patterns in Japanese Design.* New York: Kodansha America, Inc., 2001.

Hume, Nancy G., ed. *A Reader in Japanese Aesthetics and Culture.* Albany: State University of New York, 1995.

Ishimoto, Tatsuo, and Kiyoko Ishimoto. *The Japanese House: Its Interior and Exterior.* New York: Bonanza Books, 1963.

Isozaki, Arata, et al. *Katsura Imperial Villa.* Milan: ElectraArchitecture, 2005.

Itoh, Teiji. *Traditional Domestic Architecture of Japan.* Translated by Richard L. Gage. New York: Weatherhill, Inc., 1972.

Itoh, Teiji, and Yukio Futagawa. *The Elegant Japanese House: Traditional Sukiya Architecture.* New York: Weatherhill, Inc., 1969.

Iwamiya, Takeji, and Kazuya Takaoka. *Katachi: Classic Japanese Design.* San Francisco: Chronicle, 1999.

Iwatate, Marcia, and Geeta Mehta. *Japan Houses.* North Clarendon, VT: Tuttle, 2005.

Jackson, David, and Dane Owen. *Japanese Cabinetry: The Art & Craft of Tansu.* Layton, UT: Gibbs Smith, Publisher, 2002.

Jacobson, Max, Murray Silverstein, and Barbara Winslow. *Patterns of Home: The Ten Essentials of Enduring Design.* Newtown, CT: The Taunton Press, 2002.

Japan Foundation and Victoria and Albert Museum, London. *Japan Style*. Tokyo: Kodansha International, 1980.

Kakuzo, Okakura. *The Book of Tea*. Introduction by Liza Dalby. North Clarendon, VT: Tuttle, 2000.

Katoh, Amy Sylvester, and Shin Kimura. *Japan: The Art of Living: A Sourcebook of Japanese Style for the Western Home*. North Clarendon, VT: Tuttle, 1990.

Katoh, Amy Sylvester, and Shin Kimura. *Japan Country Living: Spirit, Tradition, Style*. North Clarendon, VT: Tuttle, 2002.

Katoh, Amy Sylvester, and Yutaka Satoh. *Blue and White Japan*. North Clarendon, VT: Tuttle, 1996.

Kazuo, Nishi, and Hozumi Kazuo. *What Is Japanese Architecture?* Translated by H. Mack Horton. Tokyo: Kodansha International, 1996.

Koizumi, Kazuko. *Traditional Japanese Furniture: A Definitive Guide*. New York: Kodansha America, Inc., 1986.

Lancaster, Clay, and Alan Priest. *The Japanese Influence in America*. New York: Walton H. Rawls, 1963.

Lee, Sherman E. *The Genius of Japanese Design*. Tokyo: Kodansha International, 1981.

Lee, Sherman E. *Japanese Decorative Style*. New York: Harry N. Abrahms, Inc., 1961.

MacWeeney, Alen, and Carol Ness. *Spaces for Silence*. North Clarendon, VT: Tuttle, 2002.

McClellan, Ann I. *Cherry Blossom Festival: Sakura Celebration*. Piermont, NH: Bunker Hill Publishing, Inc., 2005.

Mahoney, Jean, and Peggy Landers Rao. *At Home with Japanese Design: Accents, Structure and Spirit*. North Clarendon, VT: Tuttle, 2001.

Marra, Michael F., ed. *A History of Modern Japanese Aesthetics*. Honolulu: University of Hawai'i Press, 2001.

Mehta, Geeta, and Kimie Tada. *Japan Style: Architecture, Interiors, Design*. North Clarendon, VT: Tuttle, 2005.

Moes, Robert. *Quiet Beauty: 50 Centuries of Japanese Folk Ceramics from the Montgomery Collection*. Alexandria, VA: ArtServices International, 2003.

Morse, Edward S. *Japanese Homes and Their Surroundings*. North Clarendon, VT: Tuttle, 1998.

Murata, Noboru, and Alexander Black. *The Japanese House: Architecture and Interiors*. North Clarendon, VT: Periplus/Tuttle, 2000.

Nakashima, Mira. *Nature Form & Spirit: The Life & Legacy of George Nakashima*. New York: Harry N. Abrahms, 2003.

Nitschke, Gunther. *From Shinto to Ando: Studies in Archaeological Anthropology in Japan*. London: Academy Editions, 1989.

Paine, Robert T., and Alexander Soper. *The Art and Architecture of Japan*. Baltimore: Penguin Books, Inc., 1969.

Rao, Peggy Landers, and Jean Mahoney. *Japanese Accents in Western Interiors*. Tokyo: Kodansha International, 1988.

Rao, Peggy Landers, and Len Brackett. *Building the Japanese House Today*. New York: Harry Abrahms, Inc., 2005.

Rybczynski, Witold. *Home: A Short History of an Idea*. New York: Penguin Books, 1986.

———. *The Most Beautiful House in the World*. New York: Viking, 1989.

Seki, Akihiko, and Elizabeth Heilman Brooke. *The Japanese Spa*. North Clarendon, VT: Tuttle, 2005.

Shankar, M. K. *Worlds Within: The Japanese Home*. Hong Kong: FormAsia, 2003.

Slesin, Suzanne, et al. *Japanese Style*. New York: Clarkson Potter, 1987.

Smith, Bruce, and Yoshiko Yamamoto. *The Japanese Bath*. Layton, UT: Gibbs Smith, Publisher, 2001.

Soshitsu, Sen XV. *The Spirit of Tea*. Translated by Paul Varley and Kurokawa Shozo. Kyoto: Tankosha Publishing Co., Ltd., 2002.

Sosnoski, Daniel. *Introduction to Japanese Culture*. North Clarendon, VT: Tuttle, 1996.

Statler, Oliver, ed. *All-Japan: The Catalogue of Everything Japanese*. New York: Quarto Marketing, 1984.

Stewart, David. *The Making of Modern Japanese Architecture—1868 to the Present*. New York: Kodansha International, 1987.

BELOW: This handsome 1880s *kaidan tansu* sports a Kamakura-style finish with layers of red and black lacquer. The hanging *maru obi* is a kimono sash made of heavier silk. (Courtesy of Ming's Asian Gallery.)

Takeshi, Nakagawa. *The Japanese House: In Space, Memory and Language.* Translated by Geraldine Harcourt. Tokyo: International House of Japan, Inc., 2005.

Takishita, Yoshihiro. *Japanese Country Style: Putting New Life into Old Houses.* Tokyo: Kodansha International, Ltd., 2002.

Tanizaki, Jun'ichiro. *In Praise of Shadows.* Translated by Thomas J. Harper and Edward G. Seidensticker. New Haven, CT: Leete's Island Books, 1977.

Turner, Edward R. *Making Japanese-Style Lamps and Lanterns.* Vancouver: Hartley & Marks Publishers, 2002.

Tempel, Egon. *New Japanese Architecture.* Translated by E. Rockwell. London: Thames & Hudson, 1969.

Ueda, Atsushi. *The Inner Harmony of the Japanese House.* Tokyo: Kodansha International, 1990.

Watanabe, Hiroshi. *Amazing Architecture from Japan.* New York: Weatherhill, 1991.

Wedlick, Dennis. *Good House Parts: Creating a Great Home Piece By Piece.* Newtown, CT: The Taunton Press, 2003.

Yagi, Koji. *A Japanese Touch for Your Home.* Tokyo: Kodansha International, 1982.

Yamagata, Saburo. *The Japanese Home Stylebook: Architectural Details and Motifs.* Edited by Peter Goodman. Albany, CA: Stone Bridge Press, 1992.

BELOW: This tall 1880s *mizuya tansu* from Kyoto, made of *keyaki* and *hinoki* woods, sets off antique sake jars and a pair of 1860s bronze tigers representing the *bushido* code of warriors. The 1920s carved *ranma*, or transom panel, is double-sided in displaying its designs in two separate areas. (Courtesty of Ming's Asian Gallery.)

Young, David, and Michiko Young. *An Introduction to Japanese Architecture*. North Clarendon, VT: Periplus/Tuttle, 2004.

Japanese-Style Gardens

Albright, Bryan, and Constance Tinsdale. *A Path Through the Japanese Garden*. Marlborough, U.K.: Crowood Publishing, 2001.

Bring, Mitchell, and Josse Wayembergh. *Japanese Gardens: Design and Meaning*. New York: McGraw-Hill, 1981.

Cali, Joseph. *The New Zen Garden: Designing Quiet Spaces*. New York: Kodansha America, 2004.

Cave, Philip. *Creating Japanese Gardens*. North Clarendon, VT: Tuttle, 1993.

Chesshire, Charles. *Japanese Gardening*. London: Aquamarine, 2006.

Gong, Chadine F., and Lisa Parramore. *Living with Japanese Gardens*. Layton, UT: Gibbs Smith, Publisher, 2006.

Harte, Sunniva. *Zen Gardening*. New York: Stewart, Tabori & Chang, 1999.

Hendy, Jenny. *Zen in Your Garden: Creating Sacred Spaces*. North Clarendon, VT: Tuttle, 2001.

Hibi, Sadao. *Infinite Spaces: The Art and Wisdom of the Japanese Garden*. Edited by Joe Earle. North Clarendon, VT: Tuttle, 2000.

Horton, Alvin. *Ortho's All About Creating Japanese Gardens*. Des Moines, IA: Meredith Corporation, 2003.

Jonas, Patricia, ed. *Japanese-Inspired Gardens: Adapting Japan's Design Traditions to Your Garden.* New York: Brooklyn Botanic Garden, 2001.

Kawaguchi, Yoko. *Serene Gardens: Creating Japanese Design and Detail in the Western Garden.* London: Trafalgar Square Publishing, 2000.

Keane, Marc P., and Ohashi Haruzo. *Japanese Garden Design.* North Clarendon, VT: Periplus/Tuttle, 2004.

Ketchell, Robert. *Japanese Gardens in a Weekend.* New York: Sterling Publishing Co., 2001.

Kieran, Egan. *Building My Zen Garden.* New York: Houghton Mifflin Co., 2000.

Main, Alison, and Newell Platten. *The Lure of the Japanese Garden.* New York: W. W. Norton & Co., 2002.

Messervy, Julie M. *The Inward Garden: Creating a Place of Beauty and Meaning.* Boston: Little, Brown & Co., 1995.

Mizuno, Katsuhiko. *Landscapes for Small Spaces: Japanese Courtyard Gardens.* New York: Kodansha International, 2002.

Mizuno, Katsuhiko. *Styles and Motifs of Japanese Gardens.* New York: Kodansha America, 2005.

Nose, Michiko Rico, and Michael Freeman. *The Modern Japanese Garden.* North Clarendon, VT: Tuttle, 2002.

Ota, Hirotaro. *Japanese Architecture and Gardens.* Tokyo: Kokusai Bunka Shinkokai, 1966.

Sawano, Takashi. *Creating Your Own Japanese Garden.* Tokyo: Shufunotomo Co., Ltd., 1999.

Seiki, Kiyoshi, Haruzo Ohashi, and Masanobu Kudo. *A Japanese Touch for Your Garden.* Tokyo: Kodansha International, 1993.

Slawson, David A. *Secret Teachings in the Art of Japanese Gardens: Design Principles, Aesthetic Values.* Tokyo: Kodansha International, 1991.

Sorin, Fran. *Digging Deep: Unearthing Your Creative Roots Through Gardening.* New York: Warner Books, 2004.

Takei, Jiro. *Sakuteiki: Visions of the Japanese Garden.* Translated by Marc P. Keane. North Clarendon, VT: Tuttle, 2001.

Underwood, Penny. *Designing and Creating Japanese Gardens.* Wiltshire, U.K.: Crowood Press, 2005.

Yoshikawa, Isao. *Japanese Gardening in Small Spaces.* New York: Kodansha America, Inc., 2000.

Young, Michiko, and David Young. *The Art of the Japanese Garden.* New Clarendon, VT: Periplus/Tuttle, 2005.

Wabi Sabi and Shibui

Crowley, James, and Sandra Crowley. *Wabi Sabi Style.* Layton, UT: Gibbs Smith, Publisher, 2001.

Gold, Taro. *Living Wabi Sabi: The True Beauty of Your Life.* Kansas City, MO: Andrews McMeel Publishing, 2004.

Gordon, Elizabeth, ed. *House Beautiful.* August & September 1960.

Gordon, Elizabeth. "We Invite You to Enter a New Dimension: Shibui." *House Beautiful* (August 1960): 88–95.

Juniper, Andrew. *Wabi Sabi: The Japanese Art of Impermanence.* New Clarendon, VT: Tuttle, 2003.

Koshiro, Haga. "The Wabi Aesthetic through the Ages." *Japanese Aesthetics and Culture, A Reader* (1995): 245–47. Edited by Nancy G. Hume.

Koren, Leonard. *Wabi Sabi for Artists, Designers, Poets and Philosophers.* Berkeley: Stone Bridge Press, 1994.

Lawrence, Robyn Griggs. *The Wabi-Sabi House.* New York: Clarkson Potter, 2004.

Noma, Seiroku. *Japanese Sense of Beauty.* Tokyo: Asahi Shimbun Publishing Co., 1963.

Tierney, Lennox. *Wabi Sabi: A New Look at Japanese Design.* Layton, UT: Gibbs Smith, Publisher, 1999.

Yanagi, Soetsu. *The Unknown Craftsman: A Japanese Insight into Beauty.* Tokyo: Kodansha International, 1989.

Yanagi, Sori. "The Discovery of Beauty: Soetsu Yanagi and Folkcrafts." *Mingei: Masterpieces of Japanese Folkcraft.* Japan Folk Crafts Museum. Tokyo: Kodansha International, 1991.

A cache of wine continues aging in a custom-built wine cellar flanked by *tansu* chests, in a room where fine wine and wood celebrate the natural elements.

RESOURCES

Museums

Asian Art Museum of San Francisco
200 Larkin Street
San Francisco, California 94102
415-581-3500
www.asianart.org

The Contemporary Museum
Honolulu
2411 Makiki Heights Drive
Honolulu, Hawai'i 96822
808-526-0232
www.tcmhi.org

Freer/Sackler Galleries of
The Smithsonian
National Mall
Washington, D.C. 20013
202-633-4880
www.asia.si.edu

Honolulu Academy of Arts
900 South Beretania Street
Honolulu, Hawai'i 96814
808-532-8700
www.honoluluacademy.org

The James A. Michener
Art Museum
138 South Pine Street
Doylestown, Pennsylvania 18901
215-340-9800
www.michenermuseum.org

Japanese American National
Museum
369 East First Street
Los Angeles, California 90012
213-625-0414
www.janm.org

Los Angeles County Museum of Art
5905 Wilshire Boulevard
Los Angeles, California 90036
323-857-6000
www.lacma.org

Metropolitan Museum of Art
1000 Fifth Avenue at 82nd Street
New York, New York 10028
212-535-7710
www.metmuseum.org

Mingei International Museum
1439 El Prado, Balboa Park
San Diego, California 92101
619-239-0003
www.mingei.org

The Michener in New Hope
Union Square on Bridge Street
New Hope, Pennsylvania
215-862-7633
www.michenermuseum.org

Mingei International Museum
155 West Grand Avenue
Escondido, California 92025
760-735-3355
www.mingei.org

Minneapolis Institute of Arts
2400 Third Avenue South
Minneapolis, Minnesota 55404
612-870-3200
www.artsmia.org

Morikami Museum and
Japanese Gardens
4000 Morimaki Park Road
Delray Beach, Florida 33446
www.morikami.org

Museum of Fine Arts, Boston
Avenue of the Arts
465 Huntington Avenue
Boston, Massachusetts 02115
617-267-9300
www.mfa.org

Museum of International Folk Art
706 Camino Lejo
Santa Fe, New Mexico 87505
505-476-1200
www.moifa.org

The Peabody Essex Museum
East India Square
Salem, Massachusetts 01970
978-745-9500
www.pem.org

Philadelphia Museum of Art
26th Street and the
Benjamin Franklin Parkway
Philadelphia, Pennsylvania 19130
215-763-8100
www.philamuseum.org

Renwick Gallery at
The Smithsonian
1661 Pennsylvania Avenue NW
(at 17th Street)
Washington, D.C. 20006
202-633-2850
americanart.si.edu/renwick

Seattle Art Museum
100 University Street
(on First Avenue)
Seattle, Washington 98101
206-654-3100
www.seattleartmuseum.org

Seattle Asian Art Museum
1400 East Prospect Street
Volunteer Park on Capitol Hill
Seattle, Washington 98112
206-654-3100
www.seattleartmuseum.org

The Textile Museum
2320 S Street NW
Washington, D.C. 20008
202-667-0441
www.textilemueum.org

Antiques, Art, and Design Sources

Arai Jackson Ellison Murakami LLP
2300 Seventh Avenue
Seattle, Washington 98121
206-323-8800
Fax: 206-323-8518
www.araijackson.com

Azuma Gallery
530 First Avenue South
Seattle, Washington 98104
206-622-5599
www.azumagallery.com

Carolyn Staley Fine Japanese Prints
2001 Western Avenue, Suite 320
Seattle, Washington 98121
206-621-1888
www.carolynstaleyprints.com

Chidori Asian Antiques
108 South Jackson
Seattle, Washington 98104
206-343-7736

The Crane Gallery, Inc.
104 West Roy Street
Seattle, Washington 98119
206-298-9425
www.cranegallery.com

En Japanese Arts & Crafts
2308 Hyperion Avenue
Los Angeles, California 90027
323-660-0262

Galen Lowe Gallery
102 West Roy Street
Seattle, Washington 98119
206-270-8888

George Nakashima
Woodworker, S.A.
1847 Aquetong Road
New Hope, Pennsylvania 18938
215-862-2272
www.nakashimawoodworker.com

Glenn Richards
964 Denny Way
Seattle, Washington 98109
206-287-1877
www.glennrichards.com

Honeychurch Antiques
411 Westlake Avenue North
Seattle, Washington 98109
206-622-1225
www.honeychurch.com

Indigo
1323 State Street
Santa Barbara, California 93101
805-962-6909
www.indigointeriors.com

Japonesque Gallery
824 Montgomery Street
San Francisco, California 94133
415-391-8860

Kagedo Japanese Art
520 First Avenue South
Seattle, Washington 98104
206-467-9077
www.kagedo.com

KOBO
604 South Jackson Street
Seattle, Washington 98104
206-381-3000
www.koboseattle.com

KOBO
814 East Roy Street
Seattle, Washington
206-726-0704
www.koboseattle.com

Koichi Yanagi Oriental Fine Arts
58A East 66th Street, #1
New York, New York 10021
212-744-5577

MESH
650 Iwilei Road, #110
Honolulu, Hawai'i 96817
808-536-6374

Mika Gallery
595 Madison Avenue, 8th Floor
New York, New York 10022
212-888-3900

Naga Antiques, Ltd.
145 East 61st Street, #1
New York, New York 10021
212-593-2788
www.nagaantiques.com

Rieke Studios
416 Alta Vista
Santa Fe, New Mexico 87505
505-988-5229
www.riekestudios.com

Sebastian Izzard, LLC Asian Art
17 East 76th Street, 3rd Floor
New York, New York 10021
212-794-1522
www.izzardasianart.com

Shibui
215 East Palace Avenue
Santa Fe, New Mexico 87501
505-986-1117
www.shibui.com

The Suyama Space at
Suyama Peterson Deguchi,
Architects
2324 Second Avenue
Seattle, Washington 98121
206-256-0809
www.suyamapetersondeguchi.com

Takumi Company
Seattle, Washington
206-622-2804
www.japanesecarpentry.com

TAMA Gallery
5 Harrison Street
New York, New York 10013
212-566-7030
www.tamagallery.biz

Things Japanese Art & Antiques
800 Lexington Avenue, 2nd Floor
New York, New York 10021
212-371-4661

Tonia Prestupa Interiors
1519 Upper Canyon Road, Suite 5
Santa Fe, New Mexico 87501
505-470-5060

Lifestyle Sources

Bamboo Fencer
Custom bamboo fences, gates, etc.
190 Concord Avenue
Cambridge, Massachusetts 02138
800-775-8641
www.bamboofencer.com

Bush WoodCraft
*Custom shoji screens, fusuma, and
tatami*
841 Rainier Avenue South
Seattle, Washington 98144
206-323-2020
www.shojiscreens.com

Chado New Mexico
"Creating Peace Through Japanese Tea"
c/o Sakina von Briesen
Santa Fe, New Mexico
505-982-9395

Cherry Tree Design
Custom shoji and woodwork
320 Pronghorn Trail
Bozeman, Montana 59718
800-634-3268
www.cherrytreedesign.com

DELICArf-1
Japanese delicacies
Ferry Building, Shop 45
San Francisco, California 94111
415-834-0344

Design Shoji
Custom shoji
3000 King Ranch Road
Ukiah, California 95482
707-485-5550
www.designshoji.com

Golden Door Spa
Japanese-style destination spa
POB 463077
Escondido, California 92046
760-744-5777
www.goldendoor.com

The Japan Woodworker
Woodworking supplies
1731 Clement Avenue
Alameda, California 94501
800-537-7820
www.japanwoodworker.com

Japanese Style, Inc.
Two online shopping sites:
www.japanesegifts.com
www.cherryblossomgardens.com
16159 320th Street
New Prague, Minnesota 56071
877-226-4387
www.japanesegifts.com

Kozo Arts
Handmade books, decorative papers,
wedding invitations
1969A Union Street
San Francisco, California 94123
415-351-2114
www.kozoarts.com

Mimi-san Lipps
Japanese floral arrangement—
Nageire, Sashibana
By appointment
Santa Fe, New Mexico
505-989-4644

Miya Shoji & Interiors Inc.
Custom shoji, tatami, etc.
109 West 17th Street
New York, New York 10011
212-243-6774
www.miyashoji.com

PaperGami
Fine handmade paper
114 Tulane Drive SE
Albuquerque, New Mexico 87106
800-569-2280
www.papergami.com

PaperGami
213 West San Francisco Street
Santa Fe, New Mexico 87501
505-982-3080
www.papergami.com

Peter Lauritzen
Fine woodworking and cabinetry
POB 337
Tesuque, New Mexico 87574
505-983-5267

Shigo Kimono, Japan Center
Vintage and new kimonos
1730 Geary Boulevard, #203
San Francisco, California 94115
415-346-5567
www.asakichi.com

Shirokiya
Japanese department store
Ala Moana Shopping Center
Honolulu, Hawai'i 96814
808-973-9111
www.shirokiya.com

Stone Forest
Hand-carved contemporary
Japanese garden, bathroom,
kitchen, home
fixtures
213 South St. Francis Drive
Santa Fe, New Mexico 87501
888-682-2987
www.stoneforest.com

Sunrise Springs Resort & Spa
Chanoyu in Japanese teahouse
242 Los Pinos Road
Santa Fe, New Mexico 87507
800-955-0028
www.sunrisesprings.com

Ten Thousand Waves Japanese Spa
Japanese-style onsen
POB 10200
Santa Fe, New Mexico 87504
505-992-5025
www.tenthousandwaves.com

Uota Tatami
Handmade tatami mats
163 Tomales Street
Sausalito, California 94965
415-332-0815
www.munetaka-uota.com

Uwajimaya Food & Gifts
Japanese/Asian food and gifts
600 Fifth Avenue South
Seattle, Washington 98104
206-624-6248
www.uwajimaya.com

FACING: This is *kanji* calligraphy by artist Gail Rieke, who loves collecting heart motifs.

PHOTOGRAPHY CREDITS

Doug Merriam, principal photographer

Other photography as follows:

Bamboo Fencer, Inc., Cambridge, Massachusetts

Dale Brotherton

Jennifer Davidson

Jill and Terry Fernandez

Deborah Fleig

Golden Door spa, Escondido, California

Carl Johansen

Kim Kurian

Kimon D. Lightner

Lorig & Associates, Seattle, Washington

Robert Reck

Siddiq Hans von Briesen

Stone Forest, Santa Fe, New Mexico

Takumi Japanese Cabinetry, Seattle, Washington

Ten Thousand Waves, Santa Fe, New Mexico

The welcome invitation to participate in a *Chanoyu*, or Tea Ceremony, is silently echoed by the room's warm wood construction and natural furnishings—straw *tatami* mats and silk scrolls. (Photography by Carl Johansen.)

INDEX